YOLANDA RODRIGUEZ

An Orphan FOUND- A Memoir

How I Found My Light Amidst the Darkness And a Path to Help YOU Do the Same

First published by BreadWinnerzHHD 2020

Library of Congress Control Number: 2020925645

© Pittsburgh, PA 2020

First edition

ISBN: 978-0-578-81615-9

Editing by Celeste D. Banks- celesteb@asecondchance-kinship.com

This book was professionally typeset on Reedsy.
Find out more at reedsy.com

This memoir is dedicated to those who struggle in quiet not knowing if they can make it through one more bump in the road. It's dedicated to the nights spent alone in wandering minds and the mornings that are spent fighting to push through another day. It's dedicated to your journey and the lessons learned through the dark times.
I dedicate this to your WIN.
I dedicate this to YOU.
-with love

Until I looked within;

~Y. Rodriguez

Contents

Preface

Great morning, day, evening, or night to you!

Through the years, I have tried to write this story many times. There were always "a lot of things" that have stopped me. Just like most other times in life, "a lot of things" being myself. However, today I've decided to simply start and I want to begin with gratitude.

I am grateful for the failures that I have had in my life. There are definitely many of them. You'll hear of a few in this book. I'm grateful for the heartaches that I've faced. I'm grateful for the achievements that I've accomplished and for the stages that I've stood on, around the world, to bring joy to others' hearts.

I'm grateful for the people who've walked out of my life as well as the people who have stayed and continue to stand by my side. I'm grateful for the time my grandmother had a dinner party and my father was drunk enough to come out with his pants on his arms and head and a shirt on his legs. Yes, he was 40 years old and that really happened.

At this moment I'm most grateful for you, the one who decided to pick this book up today. There are many on the shelves. There are many online that have catchy titles, catchy pictures on the front cover, or even just relate to the words that you searched for online. You chose this one today nonetheless. That shows me that you have some form of hope for your future.

This book isn't the "save all" of books; however, it will hopefully show you that you are the "save all" of YOU! This book is not the blueprint of what you should do, step by step, to Win in your life. This is simply the journey that I took, while following a blueprint that I didn't even know was already laid out by the greats who have already won theirs .

None of us are the same. Each of us has a story to tell. Each of us have aches, memories, experiences, and feelings in our heart, that shaped us to become who we are today and who we will CHOOSE to be in the future. Each of us has a reason that we do what we do. The reason we walk how we walk and say the things to ourselves that we say every single second of every day and night is unique.

With that being said, I'm just going to get right to it and stop doing what we all tend to do when things get a little rough and scary. I'm going to stop stalling.

Let's start! I pray you enjoy it.

Acknowledgement

Many people have encouraged me along this path of releasing this story to you. Kaaren, had you not pioneered the way by writing your first book and showing me that it is possible, I don't know if I would have picked up the first pen. I thank you for reminding me that my story must be heard. Thank you for 22 years of being my twin. I thank my homegirls Rock, Kellee, and again Kaaren, who sat in my text thread through the ENTIRE writing process. You were my therapeutic outlet and support when the stories got too scary to release. You dealt with all 15 variations of my cover and gave amazing and honest feedback again and again and again and again, lol. My Awg (OG), you became my sister in one of the darkest times of my life. Your friendship and loyalty pulled me through so many lonely days and I'm eternally grateful for every minute of our friendship. Thank you for, on so many occasions, reminding me of my light. Mr. André Malone! You are a great friend and brother. I'm grateful that you were led back into my life. Thank you for simply being André. The genuine words of encouragement, jokes, truths, and the love have been a blessing for decades. Mrs. Plowey, my friend and childhood mentor, I thank you for giving me a room to escape to when my mind was in a fog in school; for being a pseudo mother to me when I needed a kind word or a lunch; for, possibly, being the one person who will catch all of the typos in this book and cringe as much as I do when I catch them in other's books, but loving me through it. Mr. Ty Smith, thank you for capturing me on days when you didn't even know that my soul was crying out and helping to show me who I truly am. You helped me through my growth in an unimaginable way. Thank you kind sir. To the author Tasha Livingston, Girl WE DID IT, lol! "Who wouldda thunk?" This ride would not have been the same without you. I'm proud of you! This is just the beginning.

My Trinity, thank you for being a continuous beacon of light. I love you to the moon and back. Thank you for your youthful spirit and for always reminding me that you are definitely the funniest person I know. Your love brings a constant smile to my heart. My son, Rondell, thank you for dealing with ALL of the women in our home and still finding a way to grow into an amazing young man. You are a precious gem and there is no one like you. Imani, oh my Mani, thank you for loving me and for giving me a second chance at being your mother. Ava, my grandbaby, one day when you're old enough to read this, KNOW that you were born with strength in your soul and that you can overcome anything. Nieko, thank you for joining our family and loving us all the way we love you. Thank you for allowing me to become your earthly mother. Thank you for loving my baby while she healed through so much along this journey. My sweet, beautiful, loving Ma'Kai. MommyYo loves you so deeply. If you ever get this in your hands, just know that I'm sending you constant love and prayers of peace. As I told you in our last conversation, I'll always be within reach when you need me and I will always be your MommyYo; ALWAYS! I love you, Ms. Tiffany Lynnette Hale. You've been my sister and partner from day one of this thing I call life. You are an amazing woman and you deserve the world. I pray that you read this and offer yourself life. You encourage me on a daily to live and love and without you, I don't know if I would have made it through it all. In your own dark, you did your best to catch a young girl who had nothing. Hug yourself for me. My earthly mother, Celeste, there's no way I could ever tell you the gratitude I have for who and what you've been to me over the years. I adore you and thank you for helping me become a woman. To my "battle," Mr. Clement, we've been doing this for 21 years now. We've, in our own ways, raised each other from being college kids to amazing parents and adults. I thank you for loving me, for sticking with me through all of our ups and downs, and for constantly being my reasonable ear and lifelong best friend. Thank you for being an amazing father to our 3 children and for ALWAYS catching them when I fell. For that and a list of reasons that are longer than this book, I appreciate you, respect you, cherish you, and am grateful for you.

My Jaxx, my love, my soulmate, my equal half and rock. I LOVE YOU! Thank you for reading through this book part by part every night almost as many times as I have and for helping me see it clearly. Thank you for staying through the dark times, through the struggle, through the confusion, and through the growth. Thank you for being honest with me and letting me know when I'm slacking on living up to my own greatness. Thank you for that very first, "hello," which changed my life forever. You are truly the strongest person I know and there is no one in the world who I'd rather ride this journey with.

There's not one of you who's presence has not made an impact on me, and for that, I will always be grateful. I pray that you read this and laugh, cry, rejoice, and heal.

Find the Author:

https://www.facebook.com/Yolanda-M-Rodriguez-104864561557879/

Email- authoryolandarodriguez@gmail.com

ig-rodriguezyo

Tawfiqshah- Cover designer- https://www.fiverr.com/tawfiqshah

Tyrone Smith- Cover photographer- blacksmithdigitalimages.com

Anita Buzzy Prentiss- Headshot- buzzyphoto.com

Chapter 1- Yin-Yang

Part i- The Perfect Piece of Chicken

*T*here's this concept in Asian culture called the Yin-Yang. It applies to all cultures but it originated around the 3rd century BCE in Chinese mythology. I believe we've all seen it. It's the circle with half black and half white waves. When you look at it closer, you'll realize that the white half has a dot of black in it and the black has a dot of white in it.

The circle serves to represent the fact that you can't know light without darkness and likewise, you can't know darkness without light. That sounds easy. It sounds like something out of any textbook these days. But here's what it really breaks down to.

You see, I was raised in a multiracial family. My mother is black and my father is Puerto Rican. My grandmother on my mother's side made THEE BEST fried chicken.

Stick with me now because this is definitely going some-where.

If you've never had true southern-fried chicken, you've probably never had the best-fried chicken. Of course, this isn't a finite truth, so please don't put this book down and start a blog about how Yolanda is biased and believes she knows it all when it coms to chicken.

For a minute, I want you to sit back and enjoy a piece of chicken with me. Close your eyes…

Now that you've finished that.

I know I said to close your eyes but that makes no sense. You're reading a book! So, follow me now, WITH YOUR EYES OPEN.

When you first hold a piece of the perfect fried chicken, you look at the color of it. It's a golden brown. It's not too light. It's not too dark. It's crispy. You can see the layers of dipped, flipped, and re-dipped batter fried on to it. It possibly still has a little bit of the oil on it if you're impatient for that first bite like most of us. The most important part is the way that very first bite feels to your soul.

A split second before you bless your palate you're hit with the smell. We can't leave all of the joy to the tongue alone. The next experience that hits you is the batter as it hits your teeth and tongue. Before you've even tasted it, you've felt the crisp in your mouth. You feel the hint of oil and flavorful juices that come out as you bite into it. You close your eyes (not you, the biter). You taste the herbs. You taste the salt. You taste the pepper, the seasoning salt if it's done right, and the garlic powder. This isn't a cookbook, so I'll just say you taste all of the different ingredients that go into that perfect marinade and batter that led to this first bite. The flavor runs through every part of this bite that touches your palate. It isn't in the meat alone. It's in all of your senses. You've seen the color and herbs in the batter. You've heard it on the plate and when you bit into it. You've felt it on your, now juicy, fingers. You've smelled it in the air. And now you've FINALLY tasted it to wake up your soul. There's a juiciness to it unlike any other fried food. The meat isn't dry. The meat isn't bland. The meat alone has flavor from the marinating process which took at LEAST a day. It touches every part of your mouth. You can't chew it fast because you want to, no you HAVE to, taste the perfection. This, my friends, is the perfect piece of chicken. If you're like me this is what you were raised on. Every bite was the perfect bite. Some of you even pulled the crispy, battered skin off to enjoy it as a treat for when the meat was cleaned from the bone.

Now, let's go to those not raised by my grandmother, which in ways can be a blessing. To you, you've experienced chicken pleasure before. You've probably explored chicken and have had joy. Your tongue is happy! There's no higher piece of perfect chicken because what you know is all you know. One day an amazing moment happens! My grandmother invites you over.

Sidebar, if she ever does, don't go because she passed away over a decade ago and it's her ghost. I know right. That's creepy!

Anyway, my once living grandmother invites you over. She says "hey we're about to have dinner. It's fried chicken," along with whatever other amazing sides she served with it. In your head, you might be thinking, "Wow, I'm excited! I'm about to have chicken. I love chicken!"

You sit down… You look at the plate and you realize the color of this chicken is a little bit different than what you're used to. The crispiness on the outside of the chicken is a little bit thicker and holds a deeper golden hue than what you're used to. You pick it up and think "WAIT, this doesn't feel like what I'm used to." It's a little flakier and a piece of the skin breaks off in your hand.

You look around the table to see if this faulty break is happening to anyone else and you notice everyone has stopped talking. "This makes no sense. This family is normally loud. I've eaten with them before and the jokes and laughter never end. What's going on here?"

You brush it off because that smell is now pulling you in. You take that first bite and… silence!

That little piece of darkness; that little piece of knowledge that you did not have before that first bite is what lets you enjoy this bliss. Had you never taken this bite, you would have thought that the perfect piece of chicken was the way you had had it for your entire life prior to this moment. Had you never tried a good piece of chicken before this, you wouldn't grasp the perfection you were now holding in your hands. IN YOUR MOUTH! But, now that lack of knowledge and that bit of darkness, let you finally LIVE!

Part ii- You can Open Your Eyes Now

This situation happens with everything that we face in life. You only know what you know until you discover that there's more out there.

A lot of people believe that children born with a silver spoon in their mouths "have it made". You know what I mean by that.

It's the children who are given everything. They're the ones who never have to suffer financially and whose parents make sure they don't know the daily struggles and pains of having to figure out how to make it in this life. Some believe that these children are happy and that they have true bliss. Many even believe that they want that life as their own.

In reality, those children may have had the same piece of chicken that they thought was great for many years and may not know what a piece of heaven tastes like. Their silver spoons have been the bandage in their existence until they one day, possibly, stumble across struggle.

Most of these children never really appreciate the magnitude of what they're given because they've never been forced to through life experiences.

Prime example... Have you ever seen a teenager, driving a high-end car? It might be a Mercedes. It might be a BMW. It might be a Corvette or even the latest model Jaguar. Chances are this child didn't pay for the car from their own hard work. He probably didn't work 40-50 hours a week while in school to buy that car. Chances are if he crashes that car his parents will get him a new one. If his parents don't rectify the situation, this child has instantly found his version of dark. He now has to find rides, or even worse, drive his parents' hand me down car.

You see, he doesn't truly understand a major "problem" so this one is MASSIVE!

On the other hand, many people could look at a girl from the hood and think that her so called "struggle" must make her cry herself to sleep every night. "I would NEVER want her life." they could argue. This is thought while not realizing that her mother is home to prepare a home-cooked meal every day.

Her family shows love with hugs, songs, and dance every night. The thought of her pain is believed without understanding the gratitude she has when she feels a clean sheet on her bed nurturing her skin. She feels this joy because detergent and hot water was paid for this month. She doesn't take these things as small victories because she has never slept on Egyptian cotton and on more than one occasion the hot water for the baths was heated in a pot on the stove. Her current life is bliss and a hand-me-down car would be a tasty bit of icing on her cake.

There are levels to this appreciation thing and the depths of light or dark you reach based on your life experiences.

Somewhere out there, there's a child who walks every single day to school, from school, to their friend's houses, to their job or jobs, if she is anything like I was. This isn't happening in these COVID-19 times, of course, but post pandemic, she's out there walking. She finds a nice car at the lot down the street. To her, that nice car is a 10-year-old car that has multiple issues. However, she prays and believes that this car will get her from point A to point B and she is in love with it.

That child has personally found her piece of light. She has worked. She has struggled. She has walked through the soles of her shoes on occasion. At the end of the day, she bought the car that she fought for.

If this child turns around and crashes her car, she knows she won't have another one coming anytime soon. Mommy and Daddy aren't coming to buy her the new one. She can't go into her bank account to replace the one that she totaled. The car that she purchased is appreciated. Her car holds value. The car shows that there is a payoff to her struggle. In her car is a reflection of the pain that she went through. This in turn, gives her car more value than the Mercedes, BMW, or the Corvette that Mom couldn't buy her in the first place. HOWEVER, this child's cheaper and less reliable vehicle holds great value in her eyes because she doesn't know the ease of a fully functional and reliable vehicle. Her light is solely measured by what she knows. Her struggle.

In the first situation, not knowing a struggle devalues the piece of expensive metal that the first child had. He knew no dark so the light wasn't as bright as it could have been from a beautiful and secure car being given to him. On the other hand, not knowing the ease adds value to the latter even though it's likely to run for fewer than 12 months. She knew no light in the dark that she faced so hustling and getting it wasn't the end of the world. Her personal hell was diluted by the lack of knowledge in the experience.

Now flip the script in both situations and you'll see something very interesting happen to these two instances. We now add knowledge (the black and white dots) to both of them.

The first child is told "The one thing I won't give you is a car. That you must fight for and earn." And vice versa, the second child is given a brand-new car of her dreams. The silver spoon fed child would very possibly find TERROR in this idea first off and flip a whole bitch. However, they'll earn a sense of appreciation for their new vehicle once they fight to get it, reducing the possibility of him being reckless with it and increasing his love for his new wheels. He earned it and that struggle gives him just enough dark to make the car shine. He knows what it's like to be given everything. Had he not known the silver spoon life he would have found this journey that he faced and overcame to be just another Monday's hard work.

The second child is left with their first misfortune of ease. The car she is given is then driven faster and if it's wrecked

"Well, oh well! I didn't pay for it anyway!" Knowing that struggle depreciates the value of ease. In her mind, she didn't work for it so it's not worth much. The dark has been given enough light to change the magnitude of the value. And that "high end ride" simply turns into just another car. It may have started with under 100 miles on it but it's lost the struggle that she's used to and now the knowledge of dark has taken away the Jaguar's "glory".

You see, silver spoons won't get you to heaven. At the same time being from the hood doesn't take you to hell. This small dot of knowledge within the Yin and Yang gives a massive perspective. The knowledge COMPLETELY changes what we hold valuable.

Knowledge created value, just like it did with that amazing bite of a piece of southern-fried chicken

- may it's chewed delicious morsels forever rest in digested pieces.

Part iii- This Story Isn't About Chicken Or a Shiny New Car, Sorry

I didn't tell you these stories to have you crave chicken nor did I tell them to have you wondering why you didn't get a car as a kid. Don't start finding another reason to hate someone from your childhood or even the person who raised you.

I told you these stories for you to find an understanding that just because your beginnings may not have been so-called "ideal", they also may not be as extremely negative as you may feel. They have a purpose for you to find your happiness because of knowledge.

Chapter 1- Yin-Yang

We all come from somewhere. Our stories may be filled with a few more spots of light. Many of our stories are filled with a little extra dark. Heck, even some of those who eat with silver spoons have a father who drinks from a glass bottle. The liquor inside is just from a little higher on the shelf.

Each of the pages in our stories does have the purpose of moving us to our next step. YOU simply have to find what these instances in your life have taught you and make those experiences your dot of knowledge.

My father Mike, My sister Tiffany, and the little cute one is me at 8 weeks old

* * *

Chapter 1 Questions- The Outer Shell

Who are you? I know that question can be used very loosely but when you look in the mirror you see who you BELIEVE you are. Are you a parent? Are you a business partner? Are you a college student? Are you a teacher? When you look at you, WHO ARE YOU?

-

-

-

-

-

-

-

-

-

When you were a child what did you want to be when you grew up. Dump all of those dreams here.

-

-

-

-

-

-

-

-

-

-

Chapter 2- Everyone's Story Is Unique

~~~~~~~~~~

Part i- Every Great Story Starts With A Great Woman.

In Mine There Were 2

I'm going to tell you a little bit about my story. I don't want you to read the story and think that I'm asking for a pity party. Trust me, I've given myself enough of those over time with the tiny violin with Irritable Bowel Syndrome and all. The point of this is to remind you that we all have a story to tell. We have a story that we can use to wallow in or to learn from. This is what I chose to learn from.

My story started like everybody else's. I popped out of my mama. Well, it didn't necessarily happen like that.

Hell, even there starts the difference. Maybe you were cut out. Maybe the mom you popped out of wasn't even yours. Surrogacy is a dope thing. Heck, I didn't even pop out. In my first picture I have marks on my head because forceps were used to twist me a little bit and pull me out. I guess that's where my granddaughter got it from…

My daughter, Imani, laboring with my beautiful grandbaby, Ava

* * *

So, we're back in February of 1981. My mother, Melissa Patricia (Patty) Johnson, laid in Magee Women's Hospital in Pittsburgh, Pennsylvania, pushing to bring her bundle of joy to life. By her side were my father and my big cousin, Larry.

Larry had heard I was coming and got on the wrong school buses coming home nearly giving my aunt a heart attack when he didn't get off at his normal bus stop. My mother had to call her to tell her where he was. That's one of my aunt's dots of darkness that she told me about later in life.

Needless to say, life was good and I was loved. I had two parents, a big sister, and a home. This lasted for a short time and this wouldn't be a good book if we stopped there.

Not long after, my two parents at home changed to a mother, Patty, and a stepfather, Ricky Bradley. No, not Ricky. Rickey Bradley. He was a cool guy in spite of his shortcoming of loving the Redskins Pro football team. We moved to Hyattsville, Maryland, and lived a few years happily. I did the normal things that a child does. I played, survived a cicada swarm, caught my parents having sex, the norm.

My mother worked for USA Today, a major national newspaper and she was stunning and bold in that skirt suit and heels that she'd wear every day. She was a dynamic woman of Delta Sigma Theta Sorority Incorporated with a Bachelor's degree; and I was blessed to watch her walk for her Master's degree when I was 5 years old. Life was good. I had family, a mentor at home, crab boils on the weekends, and after surviving the cicada swarm, they weren't coming back for at least another 17 years, thank GOD!

A few years into the move she started spending fewer days at home or work and more days visiting hospitals. Soon, she no longer worked for the newspaper. She stayed at home more days and slept on the couch on more nights. She had more important work than what she was doing at the newspaper, I guess. Her time had become more dedicated to working for her health. I didn't get that back then. I just knew that the smell of marijuana was an interesting and mildly welcoming smell that wafted out of the front screen door when I was sent to play on the porch. I was cool with it though. Her giggles after they would smoke brought a different energy to the house. It was a calming one.

My stepfather, on the other hand, wasn't taking this new found transition as easily. Other substances kept his mind at ease. He took on new roles at home and on more days than not he was left raising two young girls that weren't even his. He became our primary provider. He picked us up from the bus stop and made sure the crab broils didn't come to a screeching halt. He did this all while he watched his favorite woman in the world go from suits and high heels to scrubs and doo rags.

After we suffered the loss of our house burning down we headed back to Pittsburgh. I know the fire wasn't started intentionally. I remember the actions leading up to it, as much as a 6 year old can remember.

On the nights leading up to the fire, I'd sit and look at the reflection of the flames flickering on the walls of the apartment. The heater was probably the newest model that was available at that time. It needed to be filled with kerosene to keep it burning. My parents kept it right in the front of the living room directly next to the wicker shelf that held my small fish tank. The coils that ran across it burned so hot and red that my step father would light his cigarettes on it. They used to holler at me because when my toes got cold in the evening, I would sit entirely too close to it to warm myself. They'd say

"You're going to catch yourself on fire, Yolanda." I'd run to the couch, cuddle under a blanket to maintain the warmth of my feet and continue to watch the reflections flicker.

We kept 2 containers of fuel in the front storage room of the house. One held kerosene and the other held some extra gas for Ricky's truck in case he was to ever run out of gas at home. A lack of communication due to mental exhaustion from my step father partnered with and a cold night at home with my sister, and in an instant, all was gone.

I walked back in to the apartment with the 2 of them the following day. Of all of the smoldering black that was left of the living room, all that I searched for were my fish. The wicker shelf was disintegrated. The glass bowl was shattered and covered in ashes from the fallen pieces of ceiling. And my fish had found their resting place within the debris.

I had never experienced great loss before that day. Of course, we had to flush a few down the toilet to their graves before this time. That's a normal occurrence in the fish cycle. I was told that when you flush them, they would get returned to the streams for their families to say their final goodbyes. That brought my young mind peace. The thought of the fear that they had while their water heated and the glass broke made tears flow from my eyes like never before. There was no peace for them nor for me.

The black dot over this time smoldered for a while but it didn't cause complete destruction, even though my fish in the tank next to the blazing red heater would beg to differ.

Me as an innocent

The trip back to Pittsburgh wasn't the road trip that we imagined it would be. There were no monuments to take pictures with or scenic views and road songs to sing with Mom. My sister and I rode back with my aunt and uncle. The ones whose son loved his little cousin. I don't really know how my stepdad Ricky got back to Pittsburgh , but if he was in the condition that my uncle was in, I'm sure he was somewhere in the Howard Johnson Hotel where we stayed, nurturing a hangover before driving himself back alone.

What I do know is my mother didn't drive at all. She was medevaced from a hospital in Maryland to Pittsburgh Presbyterian Hospital because she was too sick to endure the ride. The big "C" was taking over and she needed continuous monitoring. I wish I could have ridden back with her. I hope she wasn't scared but I'm sure they gave her an experience to remember.

I moved in with my father and my grandparents when we pulled up in the "burgh". Prior to this, I had only spent summers with them so to a 6-year-old this was a MAJOR change. You would think this would help to ease me in these times. I was surrounded by family and had 3 bedrooms to choose from while still choosing grandma's bed. You notice I didn't say my sister and I moved there.

Nah, NEXT major change… She was placed with my aunt and uncle who drove us back from Maryland. She had lost all normalcy. I can only imagine her first night there surrounded by love yet being all alone.

My moving into a Puerto Rican household was a very delicate situation. It encompassed the entirety of the yin-yang within every single day. Of course, I'm sure that lies within moving into the home of any new culture on a full time basis. It was also a joy that most people don't understand. The food was exotic. Pastelillos and arroz were heaven every week. The structure of daily life was a complete culture shock alone. The get-togethers had music that I had to move my feet and hips to. The language was exciting. I felt like under my clothes I had become an instant super hero who was about to learn to speak in a code that the rest of the world would marvel at. The 6 year old mind, haha.

My father, Miguel, but everyone called him Mike, was a Vietnam veteran. He had fought in the late 60s after being drafted and was one of the few who came home in one piece. Well, at least from the outside. The only bullet he had taken through his leg had gone in and out without him even noticing until the next day and he had lived to show me the wounds.

On the inside, he had been hit with Agent Orange while in battle causing neurological damage that is still being researched over 50 years later. He had seen friends' heads blown off while running beside him through the wild terrain. He had taken lives that had no names to him. The names didn't matter in that second. It was either him or them.

After coming home from battle, he was faced with the war on drugs in the streets. That alone could change a man in that day and age. However, if you asked him how he was doing you'd usually hear "fair to middlin," so I guess he was cool.

Alcohol became his friend. It became his best friend actually. Hell, it was even more of a friend than I was to him at times. He'd wake up in the morning with his hands shaking and needed that first swig to calm them and it always seemed to help.

I remember looking under his bed on any given day and finding a number of empty bottles. His drinks of choice were cheap red wines from the bottom shelf. His daily preferences were Wild Irish Rose and Thunderbird wine. He called them Wild-I and T-Bird. They got their own nicknames just like I had. Mine was Puddin. At times when my grandmother didn't want him to leave the house, searching for a drink too early, she'd slide him one of the partially full bottles she had confiscated from under his bed to keep him around a few hours longer. She hated that he drank but she loved having him at home more than him being in the streets.

My mother had moved in down the street after our trip back from Maryland. She lived her next months with my stepfather and his family which was a blessing for me because she was within walking distance.

I was able to visit her occasionally , however each time I saw her she looked a little different. Her cheeks below her beautiful high cheekbones, that once filled her pretty brown skin, were a little less full. Her pretty brown skin had lost its luster. Her hair went from an amazing full afro to a texture that I didn't quite understand. Back then I didn't know what wigs were so I didn't realize her hair was no longer growing from her own scalp.

When I would go to visit, Ricky would have me wait outside. I would sit on the porch and wait for her to come out. Instead of her walking to sit next to me, my stepdad would carry her out in his arms so she could sit in a chair that he would set up with a pillow and white blanket. He loved her so deeply. My mother and I did not make eye contact much during those visits. She'd give me soft smiles that held sadness and would quickly end with her asking him to take her back in the house.

One day soon after the move, my mother had us all over to her mother's house for a dinner party. It was my grandmother's house who had made the amazing chicken. My grandmother lived close by so it was a walk away for my father and I. We played our made up game of "kick-rocks" all of the way there but didn't speak a word.

The get together started out as one of the best days I had had in a LONG time. Having every one of my uncles and aunts in the room with my sister and I gave us a sense of family again. Even my father was welcomed as one of the boys. All felt good.

My mother sat on the couch with her blanket on her lap watching it all and I could cuddle up next to her when I wasn't running around to see everyone. Her normally curly fro was done up in a cute little flat curled style. She looked beautiful and sat there as though she was on a throne watching the world celebrate just for her enjoyment.

Then came the reason we were all there. "The Meeting." My mother started talking while I sat on my father's lap. She told us how much she loved us all. She especially loved my sister and me. I was so happy that she was smiling again. She looked at each and every one of us. The room was quiet and she had center stage.

The next thing she told us, well, I'm not sure if it made my heart race or slowly start to drown.

The doctors had given up. There was nothing left to do. We were there so she could see us all again for one last time. She was leaving us because Cancer had won.

I didn't understand as a little girl why they had given up on my mother. Why didn't she chosen to fight to stay with me. I didn't get it. A little girl was supposed to have her mother. Mostly a mother as perfect as mine was. We weren't done. I wasn't a woman yet. Heck, I hadn't even started my period yet. This wasn't the proper circle of life you grow up hearing about.

However, we sat and heard the truth. My father holding me, my sister on the couch quietly weeping, my tears rolling. All while my mother sat in front of us, BOLD, yet dying from the inside out.

Patty and her real fro

My mother, Patty, receiving her Master's Degree

My mother and sister, Tiffany

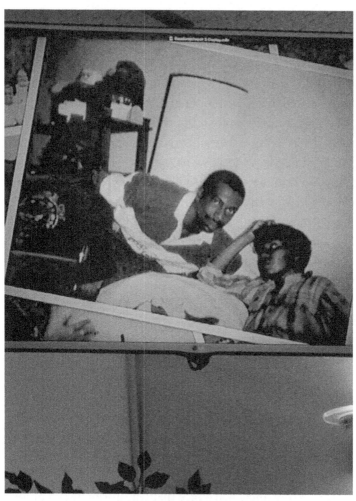

My mother with her late brothers Teddy "Ted Rat" and David the day of "The Meeting"-RIP

* * *

There's not much that I remembered after moments like that. Nothing else held that much weight in my life. All I worried about prior to that was were we going to live together again and could I get new fish. Up until that moment there were no bigger fish to fry... No pun intended my sweet burned fillets.

Time instantly stood still until the morning of August 2, 1988. I was at my father and grandparents' house. My uncle Moon came over. Moon was my mother's youngest brother, the youngest of 9 siblings. I believe they called him Moon because he was a light to many when they were at their darkest hour. I made that up while speaking at his funeral years later and I'm not sure if that was true but that's for sure how he lived his life. I wish I had known that before I started that journey with him on that morning.

Moon had come to take me for a walk up Larimer Avenue. He was carrying a T-shirt in one hand and a baseball in the other. We stopped at the baseball field, up at the top of the Ave, that was attached to the projects. We threw the ball back and forth for a while in silence. It was fun but things just didn't feel right. It felt like a chore because on that morning he looked so much like my mother. He held that look in his eyes that she would give me on the few visits I had with her on the porch. It was a loving sorrowful look of wishing every blink could hold me tighter.

You see, my uncle had a face that was normally full of love and security. He would give you this cool little sideways smirk and you knew you were about to get the biggest hug you had ever had. If you knew my uncle Moon you knew this man was an interesting, happy, silly, calm, hurt someone if they messed with his family, smooth type of brotha. He could bring peace to you through words and laughter.

On that day his face was different. He had confusion and concern in his eyes and I didn't know what it was. I think I was too young to be able to decipher emotions in others' eyes just yet. All I knew was we were playing catch and that brought me joy because he had never done that with me before. This park was normally reserved for me to run and play while my father and I were walking through it heading on one of our walking journeys to who knows where. It's the same park we cut through to get to my mother's meeting just a few months prior.

On a not so strong throw, he stopped. He came down to eye level with me to admit to me that he had been sent as the bearer of bad news. He told me he loved me and so did everyone around me. He told me that my mother's last visit to the hospital would be the last time she would see daylight. She would never walk or roll out again. He gave me the T-shirt from the zoo where my grandmother was a security guard and walked me back home. In an instant he taught me what those eyes meant. He taught me the look of sorrow. And just like, that she was gone...

My mother had died and all I got was this stupid t-shirt. I don't remember who was there when I got back home from the walk. All I could remember was she wasn't. She wasn't down the street for me to run to and tell the horrible news I had just heard. She wasn't there in the darkest moment I had ever faced. Or for any of the ones yet to come.

* * *

Part ii- Moving Forward

I saw my sister pretty often after that. I would spend nights with her and my big cousins at our aunt's house. One cousin was four years older than Tiffany, one two years older, and my cousin, Larry, the one that was at the hospital the day I was born, was two years younger. The four of them were then raised as sisters and brother. My cousin Larry was there and that was always a good treat because he loved me so much that he treated me like his favorite sister. After losing my number one woman, it was difficult to make sense of things. Being with my sister occasionally was a blessing. We were able to be alone together.

She, of course, couldn't raise me. She was a child facing her own battles so after not too long I always had to go home. From there on I continued to live with my father and grandparents and became my grandmother's shadow. She introduced me to café con leche as a welcome to my young Boricua culture. The house occasionally rang of quiet get-togethers. The living room had a glass door so if my grandfather had beer, I'd mainly just see them because "a grown-up party was never a place for kids" as Grandpa would remind me. Music played that I didn't understand because the singing was all in Spanish but watching the dancing gave me joy. In those times the black dots didn't exist.

For the next year after my mother passed, grandma kept balance in my home. Being in a home with an alcoholic father and an old-school Puerto Rican man along with a powerhouse little woman wasn't something that I can quite put into words. However, Grandma ensured she would protect my peace and heart through it all.

We'd lay in her bed and watch her daily Soap Operas and game shows. She'd show me the importance of brushing your thick hair thoroughly with the paddle brush to remove any kinks from the day while keeping it shiny. She and my grandfather were already sleeping in separate rooms, his off of hers in the back of the house, so I got to sleep with her every night.

I'd lay every night and listen to her prayers while holding each bead of her rosary. She'd pray for my father and her other 2 sons. She'd pray for my grandfather's peace. But mostly, she'd pray for me. For the nights of my crying to end. For my father to heal and be a good father to me. For me to grow up to be a strong young lady and for the damage of my childhood to never crush me. I love that woman so deeply for loving me.

I had never seen such a strong person as Grandma was. Somehow she was able to keep the peace with the beasts in our home. When my dad came home drunk and my grandfather started hollering, she told them "¡Cállate y Cálmate Alejo! (shut up and calm down Alex!) Leave my son ALONE! And the storm would instantly pass. On the days when they were quiet she taught me to snap peas and pick and preserve the beans we needed for her home cooked meals.

She'd occasionally have her friends come to visit from Puerto Rico. Our extended family from the neighborhood, the Rivera family, was always included on those events. There were smiles everywhere. It was nothing like I had ever faced in my other homes. It was at one of these parties that my father came home midday completely drunk trying to be a part of the family. It didn't take long for grandma to send him STRAIGHT upstairs. "Miguel, you will not embarrass me this time. Go upstairs and sleep it off for a while." The party kept moving. Many didn't even realize he had come and gone. Unnoticed as usual.

I can only imagine what went through that silly man's mind when his bedroom door closed behind him. 20 minutes later Grandma and I were sitting in the living room and we hear "Mama, is this better?" Her face was priceless. It's as if she had mentally jumped and seen what was waiting for her at the top of the steps and her face went completely flush white. I took off running and couldn't help but bust out laughing as soon as I hit the bottom step. She was right on my heels with a few of her guests already standing by my side.

There he was, all 145 pounds of this 5'8.5" man, at the top of the steps. Staggering, not because he was drunk. She wasn't that lucky to get that embarrassment. This time he staggered because he couldn't see. His pants were covering his arms and head and had been fastened nicely to ensure he wasn't caught with his zipper down, or I guess in this instance, up. He had on a nice sweater stretched up around his legs that, just almost, made it to his waste. And on the bottom, a clean pair of brown dress shoes to seal the deal. Oh, yeah. he was dressed to impress with nowhere to go other than right back to his room. I ran up and pushed him back in looking back over my shoulder to make sure my grandmother didn't have a full on heart attack. She was just standing there, hands on her hips. But in the corner of her lips I still saw the hint of a smile that only a mother can give to her son whom she deeply loves.

I remember, on rare occasions, my grandparents going out with their friends. It wasn't often because home was always more welcoming. One time in particular I think they were going out to celebrate an anniversary with friends. This was just a little under a year after my mother had passed. I remember my grandmother looked beautiful for this date. Her hair was done up with curls pinned on top of her head. Instead of the traditional muumuu with pockets that she always wore around the house, she wore a beautiful dress and some little pumps to give her 2 inches of height. My grandfather even put on a suit. My grandmother probably made him wear it. I remember watching them standing at the door before leaving. He was six foot two at the time. She was not more than five feet tall in heels. I had actually just passed her up in height so I often stood extra close to try and rub it in a little. Even though she was shorter in height she held her own. They were equals and I was amazed by her. They were a handsome couple.

They left smiling. I was always happy when they laughed together. That's when you saw the handsome man that my grandfather was in his younger years show through. He had a silver partial crown around the border of his front tooth and that night I swear he had brushed it a little extra because I saw it shimmering. They were in love.

My father was out doing his normal, so my older sister who was 17 at the time came over to watch me.

A few hours into the evening she got a call and then we were off to her house. YES! I got to go see my cousins again. The night just kept getting better. I went and hung out with her and did the things that you do with cousins and siblings. Monica was being a good big bully of a cousin and Dana was probably somewhere doing her nails. I loved having the extra, bonus big sisters. My sister didn't really hang out much with us that night, but she and Larry were definitely around.

The next day I came home to a full house. Elba, Olga, Hector, and my aunt Catalina, from next door, were all around. In a Puerto Rican household, there's always family there when the commotion of the alcohol was down. Only this time nobody was smiling. Me being my normal eight-year-old grandma's girl, I walked in and the first thing I did was holler up the steps. GRANDMA! Where are you? I'm home. Instantly the house was quiet. No one spoke a word.

Her Goddaughter and best friend, Elba, came to my side with that same look that my Uncle Moon had held just months before. "Hello Hunny," she said in her beautiful thick accent. I loved the way they all spoke. She sat me on the bottom step and came down to my height. "You know, your grand mama and all of us love you very much right?" I mean, of course, I knew this. Grandma was my best friend. She was helping me through the worst experience of my life. Elba didn't have to ask this. I looked around the house again "Grandma?" The feeling hit me before her train wreck of words did. "No, no mi Amor. Your grandma, she's not here. Your grandma went with God last night. She's gone m'hija…"

I instantly became aware of the reality in the room. Elba and Grandma's other friend Olga weren't there partying, with my grandmother by their sides, or making pastelillos as usual. They were there to help my grandfather make it through the next phase in his life alone. They were there not as friends to his beautiful Clara but as sisters to him…

I used to think he was a mean old man. Now, as an adult, I realize he was scared too. Probably even more scared than I was. What was he supposed to do, raising a young girl with a son who's number one love was the bottle. This isn't what he wanted to do as a grown man past middle age. This isn't how it's supposed to be.

You expect that your son will be able to take care of his own family. That's what we do in our culture. The father takes care of the home! But, Grandpa was left to father both of us alone.

He sat in the living room for the next seven days with no lights, no music, no television. He just sat in silence and mourned. He told me that this is what we do in our culture. We sit in silence after a loss and we go through the peace with our loved one and we honor their journey on to the afterlife. It gave them the freedom to become one of our ancestors and not be trapped here with grief and unfinished business.

So, I would hop up in Grandmother's reclining chair which I'm sure she had left to hold me. My grandfather and grandmother each had their own. I sat in the one that was now mine, while watching him lose his passion, and together with quiet tears shed, we mourned.

Elba standing next to my lovely abuelita, Clara

Alejandro "Alejo" Rodriguez- my grandfather/mi abuelo-RIP
(Recuerdos <memories>)

Clara Luz (grandma in heels), Alejo (grandpa), Miguel (my pops standing on 2 phone books), Angel (the oldest), y Carlos (the baby)-RIP

Chapter 2 Questions- From A Place Of Love

Who were your childhood "Angels" that you found to be your protectors? (a guardian, a friend, a teacher, a stuffed animal, a pet)

-

-

-

What did your Angels help you through?

-

-

-

-

-

Chapter 3- Release The Beasts

Part i- A Women's Size 5 Is A Tough Shoe To Fill

For the next five years, from age 8 to 13, I found myself being a little Clara Luz. If I haven't explained it yet, my grandma is Clara Luz and it means clear light. I was growing taller and in that time I grew to a size 10 shoe. But I still held the heart of that little woman who wore a size five in my soul.

I thought that when she left us my father and grandfather would love each other more. I thought they would join together and be the parents that I needed them to be to help me grow up.

However, the drinking got heavier and the fights got louder and came more often. On many nights my grandfather wouldn't let my dad into the house. He would tell him that if he came back drunk he couldn't step foot through his door.

When he said that, he meant it.

It was cool though. My grandfather owned three houses on our block. Ours was the blue shingled main house. The neighboring house was the white one he had given to my youngest uncle, Charlie. And across the street, the red brick house, this one had been given to my oldest uncle Angelo.

This is the one I would watch the rainstorms from. It had 6 steps out front that led from the street straight to the front door. I would watch the storms there with my grandfather or my dad depending on who was around. It was never with the both of them together, though. We would sit and hear the thunder rolling in and they would say, "Just wait for it." As the thunder got louder and closer you could see the house at the end of the alley start to fade away into gray. I would get so excited. They'd say "Wait Yolanda. It's coming. You see it walking down the street?" Hearing them both say that made me wonder if they ever used to do this together in better days... And there came the rain heading our way barely missing us as it passed over because of the rinky-dink green awning that covered the stairs.

This run down abandoned house was a sanctuary that my grandfather put together for the city pigeons if they were injured and needed a home to protect them from the nights. It was also a home that my father had made his own for when he needed a quiet safe place to lay when he couldn't come to our home.

He hooked it up as any war veteran would. He created a security system. There was an old coffee can with rocks in it positioned about half of the way up the steps. A string was tied around the top of it. The other end of the string reached across the steps to the banister and the string was pulled taut so that anyone trying to sneak up would trigger it to fall waking my father. Of course he taught me how to make the security system just right. The other amenities of the house I'll leave to your imagination.

On some nights Dad was able to sneak into Grandpa's house. We had a method he worked out to get him in. He would sit on the steps of the red house and whistle our secret whistle. I usually woke to the first whistle. If not, he'd make it a little louder so I'd hear the second. Grandpa's room was at the back of the house so he never could hear it from there.

I'd peek out and smile because he had made it home safely again. He would say "Hey Puddin. Where's Poppy?" If Grandpa was in the living room, dad would have me go downstairs and start a random conversation with Grandpa as a distraction.

I would ask him where my dad was or I'd ask if I could use the phone knowing it was too late for me to call anyone. He would always say no, but I'd still ask. I would ask something, ANYTHING, so that when my father walked in the door and breezed on by smelling like the entire after hours joint, the argument between them wouldn't start.

He would go to his room, get into his house clothes (because outside clothes were never worn when you're staying in your bedroom), turn on the television, and then my job was done. "Ok grandpa, I found my dad. goodnight." I'd say smiling and I'd go up and we'd watch TV together until dad sent me back to bed.

On some nights this worked. I would make my way up to my room and sleep until the next morning when he needed his next drink and it all started again. On other nights granddad was stopping him at the door, having him do an about-face and kicking him right back out the door. It was cool. He had the house across the street with the awesome security system to go to, so I wouldn't worry.

Then there were those nights in between where it wouldn't work at all. I mean, even I could smell the Wild-I coming through his pores, so on those nights I was sure Grandpa did as well. I could see it in his eyes as he let me hold the conversation. He'd try to keep his peace in front of me, but one thing you couldn't do was disrespect his home and that the smell of alcohol on my father would do the job alone.

I would make it to his room or back to bed and pray that all was clear and then the house would come alive. I never fully understood all of the words they said because many of them were spoken in a slur of Spanish, and many words came between the punches that were hitting the same mouth that the words were coming out of.

In some instances my grandfather would try to force my father out of the house physically. Maybe Dad was taking too long getting back into his street clothes or maybe Grandpa was having a rough day and felt like putting his foot down, literally. That force wasn't always easy. The two would struggle at my dad's bedroom door which was located off of the top of the steps to the second floor. On those nights they would go tumbling down the steps one over the other. If I didn't hear the hollering or wasn't there watching it all happen I'd wake up to the final BOOM! We kept ladders at the bottom of the stairs that ran the length of the hallway. They were the long ladders that had to lay on their side along the entire length of the wall. They would luckily break their fall before the two of them broke out through the wall.

My dad would leave hollering while Grandpa slammed the door behind him. Then grandpa would wait patiently, for hours at times, in his living room to make sure my father didn't come back.

I think that's when my tremors started. Being scared awake on a regular can send shivers to a young girl's heart. I would try to tell them the things that my grandmother would say to them. "Grandpa Don't hit him! Dad, just chill, just go to your room and go to bed." I'd scream over them "Why can't you two have a quiet conversation? You know I'm upstairs trying to sleep. Please, let him stay Grandpa, it's cold out there tonight. Can't you handle this like adults?"

But as a little girl in their world, my words went unheard. I was always expected to stay in my place, which as a young girl, was not in their business. Even though they had already made their business mine.

Back to my bedroom I'd run to check on my father through the window. Sometimes I was lucky, he'd be sitting on the steps of the red house smoking a Newport and I could convince him to go in and sleep it off. On most nights, by the time I'd make it back to my room he had already slipped away back into the night.

"Mike Unbothered"

Part ii- We Took To The Streets

One thing you can not do to a young girl with no mother is keep her away from her father. The streets knew my father and he would always protect me out there, so they were a safe place. With my grandmother not around, I think I was getting to the age where I believed I needed to protect him in return.

We'd try to start most of our days on the right foot. He tried to make sure I had a good breakfast in the morning. He taught me how to fry eggs and how to leave the yolk just soft enough so that my toast could soak it up from the plate as it ran out.

After we ate he had his first drink of the day, we'd leave the house and do what most any parent does who has a young girl and there was no school. We would have a playdate. This playdate was unlike the one you might think. My father's friends were all alcoholics as. They were men and women who ranged in age from 30 years to their 60s and early 70s. Many of them had children like me; stuck in the house of an alcoholic. So, those became my friends.

The adults would drink, smoke cigarettes, smoke weed, laugh, and joke their days away, while we were close enough to hear if they called our names. We would run back to them before they flipped out thinking we were ignoring them. Sometimes, this would be a room apart. Other times this would be three blocks apart. In our little neighborhood this felt safe. Everyone around knew who's kid each of us was, which alcoholic we belonged to.

In our group our parents were called winos because their drink of choice, like I said, was cheap red wine. So they knew which kid belonged to which wino. If anybody heard a child's name, within a few blocks, the parent wasn't too far away.

At 9 years of age, I knew that my father wouldn't stop drinking. I hadn't learned what the disease of alcoholism was yet, so I never knew he was deeply stuck. I didn't understand that he believed his choices to be right at the time and how he did not understand how completely wrong his decisions were. Every after hour man, bartender, and lottery runner knew my name. I was "protected," you could say.

Dad had one friend we would visit. Mr. Gates was an older man who fixed televisions. He didn't hang with the other guys because of his age so a select few would go there to sit and sip. He had to be in his late 70s early 80s. This friend stayed at home every day and he was one of those guys who would watch the block from his balcony overlooking Paulson Ave. I guess, because of his age, my father saw him more as a father who would let him drink at home and not just another old drunk.

Occasionally Dad would leave me with Mr. Gates so he could hit the streets and I was in a safe environment. That would make sense when you respect this guy as a father and friend. Dad believed that Mr. Gates was the only man who would never do my father or me wrong. So, on the days when I was too tired to walk the streets with my father, instead of seeming inadequate and taking me to my grandfather, I was left with Mr. Gates.

The guy would make me a small place in the corner beside the couch so I could lay and take a nap. I had my "own" blanket and a pillow which unfortunately smelled like Mr. Gates. When you're 9 years old down Larimer, being indoors instead of on the block with the winos, was supposed to be the smart thing to do at times.

Unfortunately, this was the place that I had my first kiss with a man. Mr. Gates would tell me he loved me and that I was safe. When people would come over and I was tired he would let me nap in his bed. When they left he'd come in and rub my hair and say that it was soft. Mr. Gates would rub other places and tell me that I was beautiful. He always said "this is our secret."

Mr. Gates lived upstairs from where I practiced with my drill team. With everything that was happening in my world this drill team was my peace. It's where I could play with the older girls and learned that I was actually GOOD at something. None of them knew what was happening right above their heads. I learned all of the steps and had solos on the team. We'd march in parades around Pittsburgh. The crowds would applaud and call our names.

When he started our private friendship, right in his backyard, drill team practice became where I learned to meditate. I know it sounds crazy to think that with everyone hollering, clapping, and dancing I would meditate? When we'd practice I'd see him watching from his balcony up above. When he recognized that I noticed him he'd blow me kisses and mouth "I love you." to me. I learned to keep my eyes forward and FOCUS! I'd stomp louder. I'd clap until my hands hurt. I'd holler to the top of my lungs. All of this until him being there disappeared from my mind. I was in my zone and at times tears would silently run down my face through the yells. What else was I supposed to do?

It's paralyzing because when your father is the only person that you have left you find every way to protect him. That included not telling him things that would make him throw an old man off of a fourth floor balcony landing himself in jail for murder.

I was my father's parentified keeper.

* * *

Part iii- ¿Y Tu?

When I was 11 years old I hit puberty. I know that's a young age but I had already faced so much at an early age that this didn't come as a shock to me. I didn't tell my father I had my first period. I used toilet paper to catch the blood for the first 2 months. When I was tired of the embarrassing moments and messes in public, I finally told him that my cycle had started and he bought me a box of tampons. I'm sure this is normal for a single father right? I read the pamphlet inside to learn how to use it by myself. I wondered for the first 2 days, why people would use the awful things. Then, I realized I didn't have it inserted properly.

Man, looking back, I get why, after my grandmother's death, my aunt went to court to take custody of me. But, Mike was all that I had and I fought by his side, tooth and nail, to stay in that house down on Maxwell Way. My grandfather taking custody of me was the best they could do with my father's condition, however, I was pleased to be in my home.

At the age of 12 my father was encouraged, by the women around him as well as those at my middle school, to enter me in a pageant. "Get the girl into normal girl things, Mike! She doesn't need to be running the streets with you all of the time. Can't you see she's growing into your son?" they would tell him.

The pageant he entered me in was called "The Miss Black

Teenage Pageant" and for my first time on stage I did an oration called "Phenomenal Woman" by Maya Angelou. "I'm a Woman!" IT FELT SO GOOD to finally "look like Patty's daughter and not Michael's son," as my aunt so kindly told me I looked one day.

I remember when he had my gown made. I was so excited to try it on. It was handmade by my classmate's mother, who was a seamstress, and I was in AWE! I felt like a beautiful young princess. I WAS that phenomenal woman. I ran in the room to show my father the day I brought it home. I showed him while I turned around in the mirror, looking at how it fit me and how I was actually getting a little bit of curves here and there. Curves said a lot for a skinny girl built like her father.

I remember him staring at me, quietly and telling me I was growing up on him. He started to cry while he looked at me and my worry that I had done something wrong stopped my twirl in its tracks. When I asked why he was crying, all he could do was tell me, again as he often did, that I was growing up so fast on him. He sat and cried to himself for a while and I went back to my room and put on jeans and T-shirt that I always wore. I guess we weren't ready for me to grow up just yet.

For the next few months following the pageant, my grandfather started to tell me that I couldn't hang out with my father as much on the nights when he came in drunk. I wasn't allowed to sit in his room and watch movies with him. He'd tell me that "a young girl has no place laying in the bed with a man, even if it is her father." I didn't understand.

One day it started to make sense to me. My father realized I was coming into the age of sexuality. He had no clue how to teach me about what was happening with my body. He drew pictures of body parts and stuttered as he described how babies were made. He used words like "privates" and "the birds and bees" so as to not use the wrong words and offend me.

I guess he thought I wasn't getting it because the best way he felt that he could teach me was by introducing me to his private parts. He pulled his pants down and asked me to look at it. He told me to touch his penis. Hold it. I remember him starting to cry again as he pulled his pants up and quietly sending me to my room.

My grandfather continued to tell me how it's not good for a young girl to hang out in the bed with her father as she hits this age. Not long after, on a drunken day or 2, I found my father's hand in places that his long, long, long lost friend had once touched. Places that made me uncomfortable, yet this showed me a sense of belonging and love.

I didn't quite admit to myself that moments like that weren't supposed to happen. I knew that it wasn't what you told to the world, but I didn't get the darkness within it. However, to keep my grandfather protected by not landing Grandpa in jail, I never told. These 2 men were all that I had and I couldn't lose them. I quickly realized that my grandfather's warnings were very overdue for my ears and heart to hear.

My trips out with my father were fewer and with more time in between. He would go his way and I would go mine. As long as we both showed up at home at night we were both happy that we were still alive. My grandfather believed that, even though I was in the streets, I was near and protected by my father the whole day.

My father's friends changed from alcoholics to those with fewer bottles and more needles over time. My family didn't know that but I paid close attention. Those were the friends who started his journey to the end.

Part iv- Silent Night

One morning, my grandfather told me that he was walking me to the bus stop. This wasn't normal, it made no sense to me. Everyday my father and I had a routine before school. We would get up, we would start our day and he would walk me to the bus stop. Even on the mornings when he had been kicked out the night before he'd be back in the morning to walk with me.

On that morning, my grandfather and I walked down Maxwell Way together. It was a quiet walk. My grandfather walked a little ahead of me with his hands in his pockets.

I noticed that there was a spot in the middle of the street. A few of them actually. He slowly walked past them until I called him back. "Grandpa, what's this? It looks like blood. Is that blood?" I asked. He looked at it for a few seconds and told me he didn't know and kept going. A lot of his generation looked at our streets with that same drained look in those days because of what the neighborhood had become.

By the time I was 12 years old, seeing blood on the streets of our blocks had become a normal occurrence. Crack, heroine, cocaine, and a few other drugs had hit the streets of our city hard. These drugs in turn, introduced a large amount of gang violence. Young boys and girls were taught, at an early age, to "rep your set." Gangs took unofficial ownership of certain blocks and corners as their own and they used these blocks as their own personal real-estate to run their businesses. Others, trying to sell to their customers, or customers not paying off their debts brought about the blood that we were forced to get used to. Even wearing the wrong color on those blocks could land anyone in the hospital.

We knew that our open fields were littered with needles from the addicts. The dealers used small, colored balloons to package their drugs in. This was they could hide their poison in their mouths without having direct contact with it. They were safe. These balloons littered our open fields. Many of the fields were no longer used for play because the back sides had become a haven for the addicts to do their drugs without the cops seeing them. One prick from their littered needles could send us to the hospital with diseases that they openly shared stick by stick. The back streets weren't to be traveled on alone because of the risk of being robbed. My street was one of those, so the blood that morning didn't largely phase me.

I didn't think of it again until I came home and saw it right there. A little darker, but still there nonetheless. "That's definitely blood!" I thought. I had seen it on my legs and arms before after falling off of my bike. I saw how it looked on my clothes later after it had dried up. YUP, that was a LOT of blood on our block. Then, I just let it go. Pops had taught me that "what wasn't my business as a problem, wasn't my problem to fix on these streets." That was one of the best ways to stay alive.

Instead, I did exactly what I did every single day. I came home, threw my book bag in my room with homework being the last of my priorities, and I hit the streets. That's what my daddy taught me to do so that's what I did.

I walked by the normal houses that I always did and said "Hi."

to the normal people. This was our routine right after school until we parted ways and this time I was free to do it alone. My grandfather had trusted me so I felt good. My father must have had me on the right path, I thought.

One guy, a young light skinned guy who was probably 18 years old, was standing on his corner house porch that day. He hollered from the porch at me "A Yo. Where's your pops at? I haven't seen him around today." That sort of rubbed me as odd. He NEVER asked me about my dad. However, at the time, it didn't really matter. I told him I didn't know and was heading to find him now and I kept on walking.

I searched at the normal places. I checked the "hole" which was a wooded area Dad and his friends had made to sit and drink while still being able to see the neighborhood. He wasn't there so maybe he was at Mr. Pat's house.

Mr. Pat was a man in his later years who had become an entrepreneur by serving drinks in his kitchen to the local alcoholics. Drinks ranged from Dixie cups for $2 to full fifths that most of the guys couldn't afford. Dad wasn't there, either. I gave up and sat on my friend's porch to hang out. At least here he knew where to find me since I couldn't find him.

As it got darker and later in the evening, my grandfather pulled up in his baby blue 1970 Chrysler Imperial LeBaron 4-door and told me to get in. WHY he had to embarrass me by making me go home before my friends was always so far beyond me, but I was getting hungry so I listened. He'd feed me.

Instead of heading down Maxwell Way he took me to Shadyside Hospital. I was confused. He didn't even feed me first but I knew he would when we left so I was in for the journey.

He walked me to a bright room and I saw my father sitting there. Half of his head was shaved and from under the bandages I could see that his face was blue and purple. His one eye was swollen closed and yet he cracked a smile when he saw me to help ease the moment. He said that under those bandages were 14 staples. I stood, frozen, afraid to touch him. I didn't want to break him any further. I couldn't risk being the one who made him leave with my mother and grandmother. So, I stood back and watched until he reached out for a hug. For a while we sat there and wept, both of us feeling blessed knowing how close we had come to not seeing each other again.

I later heard more of the story about that night. I don't even know if they would have told me the full story had my cousin not come over to visit me from next door. She was my uncle's daughter and she brought that cute little poodle, Baby, over to play with me. Baby found my father's bandana that had somehow slipped under the couch in the commotion from the night before. It was covered in the same blood that laid in the puddles in the street.

Recently, my father had been hanging with one of his Cuban friends who had become more like a brother to him and a part of our family. His friend owed that young guy on the porch money for drugs. On that particular night, probably after the instigation of my loud/no back down father, that young punk and his friends decided it was a good night to chase my dad and his friend home. They beat them all of the way to the end of my street where that puddle pooled.

My father did what he felt was right to keep me safe. He went to the neighbor's house. The neighbor to the other side of us, who was my grandfather's younger brother, Uncle Pete. I was told that my Uncle Pete brought my father home, knowing that there was nothing that he could do for him from his house. He carried him in and laid him on our couch.

This all happened while I was asleep on the third floor. Baby was with him when he came that night. The paramedics were called and were told to not use their siren so as not to wake me. They treated him the best that they could and rushed him to the hospital. He had suffered broken bones, a few cracked ribs, a black eye and a fractured skull. They were surprised he had survived the beating with the amount of blood loss.

A couple of dollars for drugs almost left me fatherless. The world was failing me.

My father stayed in the house for some time after that. I don't know if it was because he had to heal or because he was scared to go back out. Either way, I had my dad back. He drank less. He couldn't go cold turkey of course because that withdrawal on top of his injuries would in fact have killed him, but it was less.

He started to regain his health and for the first time in years he began to gain weight outside of his beer belly. His skin began to look radiant. His smile was clear and the dark spots around his eyes, outside of those from the fractured eye socket, were fading away.

But the streets always called to him. Not long after taking his first steps outdoors, the streets were his home again. Alcohol became his primary love and I was once again pushed to the side.

To think, that boy asked me where my father was that afternoon when in reality he wanted to know if he had killed him. It left a pit of fire in my stomach for decades to follow.

* * *

Part v- These Streets Love No One!

Those preteen years were filled with a lot of death. Being raised on the streets of Pittsburgh in the middle of the 90s meant every moment of every day was a part of gang violence. I knew which streets not to walk on wearing blue. I knew that wearing red in my neighboring neighborhood could result in me being shot. I also knew that if you were from my neighborhood, the only safe color was black. Within the black "hood" streets there were pockets of yellow, green, and white as well, but the mutual color was black. It was my safe zone.

A new face being painted on a wall told me that the war coming for the next month or so was deeper and to be extra aware of slow riding cars. I knew that the face on the wall meant that more faces would soon be added to it, if not in my hood than in someone else's due to a retaliation kill. One summer we lost five guys that I know of, in our part of the neighborhood alone. All of them fell to gang violence. Some right on their own street when they were trying to get home. Another even took his last breath at the back door of his own home. They were friends, who later joined each other past the pearly gates at the crossroads. One of them was my cousin. Scooter was a good guy who was on a good mission that day. It felt like everybody in the streets loved him. He had an amazing smile that would light up a room and beautiful hair that all of the girls wanted to touch. He loved his little sister and would do anything for her. Even on that day he was on a mission to show her that. Yet and still, he also loved the streets and the streets didn't love him back.

On the morning of February 2, 1995 I sat at my cousin Denna's house getting ready to attend a funeral for one of these young men.

Denna became more like a sister to me after my grandmother passed. Her mother lived in walking distance and was one of the unofficial mothers to all of the lost children. Heck, hers was even the house we all went to stay at after my younger cousin caught chicken pox just so we could all catch it and gain our immunity.

The young man that we were burying that day was a football player. D wasn't a gangbanger. He was something like me. Our friends chose to love the streets a little harder but they were all we had, so they were our brothers until the end. Like any other night he went to Wendy's with the guys; however, on that night he did not make it back home. The streets loved no one.

As I was putting on my black funeral clothes, yeah we had those, there was a phone call. Back then we didn't all have cell phones. My cousin took the call on the house phone and told me, after hanging up, that it was my mother's sister, Aunt Gracie. She was calling to tell me that my cousin Rita from my father's side had come by her job looking for me and was on her way to pick me up.

It was as if one side of my family could never just let me be with the other side. I had a funeral to go to to pay my respects to this young man from a neighboring neighborhood. I didn't want to spend time with Rita that day because I was spending time with my other family. My street family. A funeral for one of the boys is a common thing that you attend. When you were a young girl from my neighborhood this was what you all did as a unit. You don't leave your family hanging during that time. It was a show of respect and it gained you respect from those around you at the same time.

However, I was only 13 years old, so I listened and was back in my all black tee, jeans, and black hi-top boots before she got there. When she knocked on the door I answered.

And there they were again! Those damn eyes were staring at me. I hated those eyes. I instantly tucked that thought deep within my core. I would never have those feelings again, for sure. It must have been a feeling from the funeral that we were about to attend sitting in the back of my mind playing tricks on me. Everyone carried that look those days.

She said. "Hey little cuz. They found your father this morning." This could only mean he had fallen asleep again in the field down the street. The cops must have found him sleeping and took him away for trespassing. It wouldn't be the first time. I told him to go to the red house but sometimes when the world was spinning from too many drinks, the stars were the best thing to keep him calm through the night. Here we go, off to pick him up from the drunk tank at the courthouse.

"So, okay, where did they find him this time?" I asked her. She told me "They found him in his bed," and that he was gone forever. I remember trying to run from her, from reality. Denna's was a small house so I left the living room and ran through the dining room landing on the kitchen floor when there was no room left to run. The walls were spinning around me. How could I possibly lose my protectors from the dark in my mind, all within a seven year time span? Who was I supposed to go to now? I was heading to a funeral one minute, then learning how to plan one, the next. How could I possibly now be an orphan? The room just kept spinning until I saw Rita standing over me with her hand reached out saying "Come on, cuz. Let's go home."

I again came back to my grandfather's house with that same

empty quiet feeling. I was completely tired of walking into this house by this time. The pain made me cringe just seeing the hallway. This time, standing in the house were my grandfather and my uncles Charlie and Angelo. They didn't have much to say to me other than to give me a hug. I guess in reality, after losing their mother Clara and my father, they needed a hug in return. I was all they had left of him. He had left me to quickly grow up and be their support while they tried to be strong for me.

They let me go and I went to my room. I didn't go into my father's room for days after that. I didn't want to see if there were marks on the ceiling. He always told me that since my room was above his, if he'd ever need help he'd bang on the ceiling with his cane to get my attention. I wondered if he even knew I wasn't home that night.

I never looked at the ceiling to see if he tried. They told me that my father passed peacefully. That Grandpa had gone in to ask him something at 6 in the morning and when he tried waking him he was asleep like a baby, never to move again.

When I did go to his room days later I saw all of the answers that I needed. His room was the same as usual except for his nightstand. On it, there was a paper towel covering his normal ashtray. I lifted the paper towel to find his needle sitting comfortably in his ashtray replacing the usual cigarette butts that I was used to seeing there. My father had OD'd while trying to run away from the pain. I can't say if it was a drug overdose, a final succumbing to alcohol, or a mixture of both. I just know he had finally OD'd on life and I'm sure he was grateful to be free. Still, I never looked at the ceiling.

His wasn't the funeral I was supposed to be thinking of on that sunny winter day.

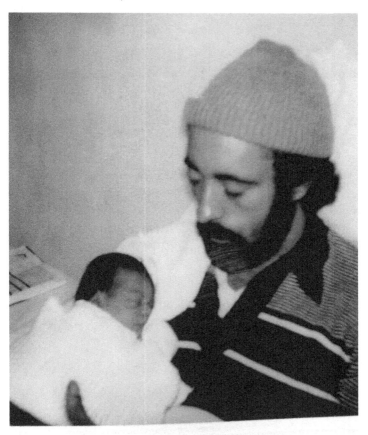

Pops and I when I was 4 days old

**A1C Rodriguez-Center-Air Force Photography
unit-Vietnam War- 1969**

Miguel Victorio Rodriguez-Westinghouse High School Class of 1966-Senior Picture

* * *

Chapter 3 Questions- Hello Inner You. I'm Listening...

I told you my story to open your heart. I wanted to have a conversation with your child within you. Usually this child is hiding behind blame, guilt, or avoidance. However, you're still there and I'm glad you came out to join us. Namaste, The divine in me respectfully recognizes the divine in you.

What situations in your life is that inner child sitting behind? What are the "If only my mother would have" or the "If I wouldn't have had... happen to me", maybe even the "If I didn't look like (...) then the other kids wouldn't have..." situations you are holding onto ever so dearly? The ones that you are holding onto so much so, that they are hindering your growth? Talk to me, inner child.

-

-

-

-

-

–

–

–

–

–

–

What do you believe those situations and events are holding you back from today?

–

–

–

–

–

–

–

How are they holding you back? (mental health, alcoholism, fear, etc....)

-

-

-

-

-

-

-

-

'

Chapter 4 - Let's Fast Forward

Part i- The Next 4 Years Were A Blur... Kind of

I was blessed to have my history. I know that sounds crazy after what you just read. Nonetheless, before I even knew what the Yin-Yang was, I believed that there had to be a reason for all loss, pain, fear, and emotional struggle. I still believed that I could make it through life in one piece with both mind and body connected. Until this day, even after the bull shit I that I've lived through, you'll hear me say "Everything happens for a reason."

Friends and associates have asked, "Oh yeah? So, your mom died when you were seven years old leaving you in a house that brought more pain than pleasure. What was the reason for that?"

I explain to those who ask that had my mother not passed I never would have had the opportunity to meet my grandmother in the way that I did. I mean, I used to spend summers with her, but I never got to live with her, on a day to day basis, throughout the rest of the year. I never would have realized how strong she was. I never would have spent cold winter nights with her curled up under her blankets had I not had that year with her. I was not old enough to have café con leche with her before that year. I probably would not have had a chance to learned how to stay strong and keep my footing while things around me seem to fail. I never would have learned how much she loved my father and my grandfather. I never would have seen unconditional love.

People may then ask "What was the reason for her passing? Why didn't she stay to teach me her cuisine or her language? I explain that her purpose was served. I had to practice what she taught me while it was fresh. She showed me love while standing her ground which helped her keep her sanity and elegance. I watched it day in and day out. She taught love, strength, endurance, and resilience and died while I was young to ensure that I did not have to watch it carry on with her for decades to come. I'd explain that seeing what my father's mother lived with showed me that she was due for her own peace away from the lions' den.

One might ask me, "Your father passed less than seven years after your mother. Just 17 days before you turned 14. What was the reason for that since you believed he was all that you had left?"

To that I'd explain how the streets might have made me. But, can you imagine how life would have been if I would have stayed down there and let the streets take me? My father's death taught me that he wasn't all that I had left. His passing introduced me to myself through seeing that I was all that I truly had left. I now understand that those years added value to who I am. They gave me the mentality of, what doesn't break you has the capacity to make you stronger. Those memories and lessons helped me through the many things that I faced as an adult. The rainy days that I face, come with a sweet memory of that porch with my grandfather. The deaths that I live through, no longer feel like they are the end of the world because I've learned that there are always bright days that follow. When my father passed my neighborhood was failing. It had a fracture in it that could take even the brightest and strongest person to the pits of the black that we all wore. Rainbow balloons being used as baggies for poison wasn't a thing I needed to stay a part of first hand, day in and day out. Unfortunately, it was time for me to grow up and move away from my home. With that, he left to allow me to soar freely.

After Dad passed away I did what my grandfather taught me. I sat in silence for a while, no TV, no radio, and no friends. I reflected.

I had to make a decision. Did I follow his path on the streets because that was what I knew, or did I follow what was in my heart and soul which kept telling me to keep going? Keep going the way I had kept going after my mother passed away and after Grandma's heart failed her that night.

It was then that I decided that I had to keep going. If living through losing them didn't take me out, I wasn't going to allow my own self wallowing to do me in.

My first job was to get out of middle school.

I was half way through 8th grade and I had no one left who was going to walk me to the school bus in the morning. I had already gotten used to the other little girls, who didn't know my life, teasing me. They teased about my hair for not being fried up like theirs because I was doing it on my own. They teased about the clothes that I wore because most of the girls did not know what it was not to have "Mommy" shopping for you. They teased me for being the "stinky girl," not getting that no one had taught me feminine hygiene or how to shave my underarms. They teased me for a lot of things that made me learn to turn a blind eye to the pain. I was able to ignore the pointing and faces they gave. I learned that their judgement couldn't kill me. And I learned that none of them had offered me a day's meal so their opinions of me belonged in the trash along with their immature personalities. Those days and words encouraged my strength while letting my trust slip away. I had to get through this part alone.

Even those days had a reason. As an adult, I've used their words to learn forgiveness. Many of those girls are still in my life. They smile at me and offer me their form of adult friendship. They've showed me how people can change and from that I've embraced forgiveness of them and others. The forgiveness is extended even when they haven't asked for it. (Don't worry ladies, you aren't about to see your names listed so the world hates you for messing with the lost girl. Just know that I remember and I do forgive you.)

For some time I continued to spend my days down Larimer Avenue, hanging with my friends or just being in the environment that I was comfortable with. My nights were spent 3 miles away in Wilkinsburg. Thank goodness my sister now lived in my hood's "sister" neighborhood. At least there they still wore only black so my wardrobe was not a thing during my commute. Another hidden blessing, right? It also made it "safe" for a guy from my hood, an older friend of mine named Dave, to catch the bus with me at night so I wasn't walking the streets alone. In the mornings he was also safe there, alone after he walked me to the local public bus stop to head off to school.

Now, actually being in Wilkinsburg was a different story. I can't say that it was any more safe. I can't say that I saw any less violence. Watching young men and women being initiated into the local gang was still the same scene of them standing while taking a beating from multiple men and never fight back. In the end they'd hug their abusers thanking them. I'd watch guys and girls go through this same act on the side streets. That's just crazy now when I think about it but at the time it was a thrill to see them pull through with courage.

Not long after 9th grade started, my grandfather, or maybe I, made the decision that I must stay with my sister in Wilkinsburg full time. With the emotional disarray we were both in it was probably easier for him not to have a young girl who was hurting and rebelling to raise, while he was going through his own mourning process of loss. I understand that more clearly now, after years of hating him for letting me go.

My sister's life had changed a lot by then. She was no longer living in Penn Hills with my aunt. She had 3 children and was soon pregnant with her forth. She had a fiancé who adored her and she found comfort in the hood. Well, maybe not comfort exactly. In reality, it was probably the only place she could afford at the time, with 3 kids, working the typical 9 to 5. But, this story is not about her, though. I'll let her tell hers in her book, because I know she has a story to share that I can not even imagine. She is simply a woman in a different page from this world who is still living her own narrative.

But this book is not about every detail. It's not about me trying to sleep through my middle school graduation day nor my amazing, middle aged, balding, white counselor showing up in the middle of one of the most dangerous neighborhoods of Pittsburgh knocking at my door and making sure I went to that graduation.

I had prayed that I would sleep through that morning and I knew that waking my sister to go with me was a fight that I would not win. She slept through that day just like she slept through many of the other days that I needed her.

While I dug through her clothes to find something to wear I watched her. Her breathing had already changed showing that she wasn't asleep any longer and that little rock she would do when her mind was racing waved slowly under her blankets. But saying anything would have fallen on deaf ears, so she and I both pretended to let her sleep in peace. Instead I kept focus on searching for the least wrinkled outfit that I could borrow from her to get me through this last day of the kids teasing me.

I would love to sit and tell you more about the things that I went through. I could release it all once and for all. However, this book isn't solely about the pain that I faced. It's not about the new guy that I temporarily found who was 19 years old when I was 14 who had made me feel comfortable in this new environment. It's not about the hangovers, the roaches, or the times we went without utilities. It's not about my father's Vietnam Veteran's burial flag being lost with the our household items that were thrown out during one of the evictions. Nah, it's not about any of those things.

* * *

Part ii- In High School High

Over the next four years, life continued. With its ups and downs like anyone's high school years. My father had already introduced me to Newport 100s. I guess I had become a lite version of an alcohol produced rotten apple that hadn't fallen too far from the tree.

On the few days that I wasn't working one of my jobs, my evenings would often be filled with spades games with my friends who were in their 20s accompanied by 40 ounce bottles of beer, a few blunts, and a pack of squares that lasted us jointly maybe 2 days. It helped keep me off of the block so I didn't complain.

With there being little ones in my house, a brother in law that had walked out one day never to return, and a sister fighting her own demons, my focus was concentrated on helping my nieces have another parent in the house instead of being parented myself. Those days were gone and it was time for me to again, grow up.

Starting in the 9th grade I continuously worked 3 jobs to make sure I ate and could help provide for some of the little ones looking up to me. A typical work day began directly after school. I worked with AmeriCorps until the office closed at around 6pm. I'd go straight to my second job at McDonald's and would work until close of business. This would sometimes be closer to 1am instead of when the doors locked at 11. On the weekends I'd work mornings at the bank opening envelopes to make sure the bills and the checks enclosed matched and had all of the needed details .

I was able to attend Peabody High School by joining the color guard team before the school year started. It wasn't my home school but it was a school where I felt most safe. I had my cousin Denna there as well as the boys I had grown up with hanging on Collins Avenue. It was a school where wearing black was still safe in the flood of red, as opposed to my home school where if you weren't in blue, getting home was less likely.

Throughout those four years I participated in and loved the color guard. I became co-captain in my first year. I ran track and was pretty good at it. I founded a step team that helped many other young girls and guys have something to do after school to keep them off of the streets. I was also encouraged by my English teacher and my twin-best-friend to join the musical theater department where I found it possible to disappear into the stage world in my mind. I would vanish just like back in the drill team. My old form of meditation was once again my peace.

Needless to say, these things cut back my work hours on many days but it gave me a safe space to be normal so it was worth it. I played Auntie Em in "The Wiz" one year. I also danced as the yellow brick road in the same musical. I became the lead dancer in "Guys and Dolls" the next year. I guess hanging with my dad taught me something because in the grand finale I was the lead male dancer wearing a fake mustache with all of my hair tucked up into my Kangol style hat.

My senior year musical was the highlight. I played Rizzo, a pink lady in a remake of "Greece" with my best friend, Kaaren (like CAR IN), playing the lead of Sandra D., dancing and singing side by side with me.

Through high school I faithfully went to youth groups and bible study to sing to a God that I wasn't sure even loved me but I was free there to dance and fellowship while receiving a weekly, home cooked, nutritious meal.

With a good daily dose of marijuana I lost myself in that school and the many programs as I began to find myself at the same time. The streets didn't seem as important to me even though they did follow us behind those brick walls.

The yearbooks carried pictures of that young man whose funeral I was supposed to go to back on the day that my father died. A lot of kids in my school see that and they mourn for him and they miss him. I see his face and I'm one of the few outside of his family who remember the exact date of his funeral, because it's a day that my world had once again changed.

I remember the riots in the halls with the gates locked down and the homie Spoony punching the dean in the face. I remember the young girl who committed suicide over a broken heart, dying in her sister's arms. I remember one of the stars of the football team trying to pick a fight with me on the streets, not realizing that I had friends from the streets too, which caused his actions to change very quickly back into peace and calmness towards me.

Through high school I met another one of those guys who was too young to be my father; however, he was at the right place to be a shoulder and ear. Mar didn't wear black everyday and at times that induced fears in me that many wouldn't understand. I faced threats from the same guys who jumped my father when they saw me in the streets with Mar. I tried to get the boys from Wilkinsburg to welcome him around without harassment which was more trying than he knew. He was good for me so I made it happen in spite of his addiction to wearing red and camouflage. To him I'll forever be grateful because, for that short time, I was no longer facing the world alone. In those few years with him I learned the value of using the phrase "why not?" When I was being faced with something that I could do, that others would ask "but why?" to the attempts, I started to reply to the world with the response "Why not?"

When we moved to another house practically with the onset of every school year, I thought "oh well, why not? It's a new experience right?" When everything that I wore for those 4 years came from my own hard earned money instead of the help of the adults around me, I'd say "Well, why not? At least I'm not getting teased for what others had me dressed in." When the kids in my house weren't going to have a Christmas and I chose to use my checks for a tree, decorations, lights, and gifts for the family I thought "Why not? Them having a beautiful morning to wake up to was worth my eating less for the next two weeks. Even though I was still a kid myself I was too old to need anything under the tree for me."

I know that wasn't his intention when he taught me that phrase but it helped me sleep at night.

A long four years after my father died I did what most thought I would not. I walked across the stage as a graduate with my diploma from Peabody High School on time! I'm not saying that I did it gracefully. Schoolwork was the last thing on my mind which landed me at the bottom of my class at graduation. However, I still graduated on time and that was a major achievement for a girl like me.

My getting out of high school didn't mean that I got to find my dream job. I wasn't excited about the paper that I could now carry showing that I had completed. It didn't excite me because I could tell people that I had finished on time.

Leaving high school meant that I could now leave Pittsburgh! I was worthy to go to college. I had done my best to walk that stage and leave my past behind me. A place that was miles away from the blood that soaked so many of the back streets.

Kaaren (Sandra D.) and Yo (Betty Rizzo) in our senior musical in Mrs. Plowey's class- Rm 219

* * *

Chapter 4 Questions- Survival Mode

What were some of the escape tactics you used in your younger years to dilute the negative things you were experiencing, literally or mentally?

-

-

-

-

-

-

-

-

When you left your childhood home, either physically or mentally, headed towards your next goal, what was your BIG plan? I'm not asking you what you wanted to be when you grew up. I'm asking what you were truthfully going to do?

What, from your past, were you grateful to finally change?

If you haven't left yet, what is your plan? What do you want to make different in your next chapter?

-

-

-

-

-

-

-

How does that plan differ from where you are now or does it?

-

-

-

-

-

-

-

If you are not where you planned to be, do you believe you are more pleased with your current circumstances or do you feel like you failed that goal?

If you haven't started that path yet, what's an alternate outcome you will be pleased with if life doesn't go exactly as planned?

-

-

-

-

-

-

-

-

Who do you blame/congratulate for those plans working out or completely flopping? What was your role?

-

-

-

-

-

-

-

-

Chapter 5- Just When You Thought It Was All Over

Part i- Leaving Isn't The Heal All

*Y*up, that was the best fast forward that I could give you of my childhood without drowning you in my mess. I'm not the only one with a rough background and I don't want you lost in feeling sorry for me and forgetting the purpose of why I wrote this book.

Of course, good things happened within there. My dad taught me how to fix a bike and I would ride on my block under the streetlights for hours scaring the crap out of my grandmother because of the little dirt hill I would race down.

I spent time sitting on the porch with my grandmother. On weekend mornings, the produce man drove up and gave us fresh fruit to eat while he and Grandma spoke in their native tongue and I'd listen in awe having no clue what in the world they were saying. I always received free fruit for being the "sweetest little thing."

My grandfather taught me to love birds and how to feed them directly on my lap. People in the neighborhood would call Grandpa the pigeon man because they'd ride by and one would just be sitting on his lap like THAT was normal.

He also made sure that when I was very young I learned a little bit about the basics of Spanish and how to speak it "in OUR accent," as he would say. Let me tell you, Puerto Rican culture is a proud one and I love it.

It wasn't a complete dark space. I shared these particular stories with you to get a point across. I didn't want to point out that I needed help. I didn't need help from anyone. And that's exactly where I'm going with this. In the end, feeling bad for myself was part of my problem until I decided to stop. I tell you this so that you can realize that we all have a story that we can stop living.

I thought when I went away to college, my rough patch of it all would end there. I would go to school, get the degree, get the job, and I would live "the life"; period. Well, that didn't happen quite as expected or in that order.

My first semester at college, out of habit, I put myself right on the educational probation list. After doing the applications for school and financial aid alone and then borrowing the last $500 I needed from a friend's mother to get in to school, my goal should have been to focus my mind on school.

But as we know, that's not why I left my city. My heart needed to get away and to stop facing my past anymore. I did that through partying, drinking, and sleeping way too late on class mornings.

By the end of my second semester of college, I had reached

for many guys trying to find love, attention, affection, I don't know... maybe I was looking for a yet another father figure.

Well, I found a father but not for me. I was 19 years old and I was pregnant with a guy from Philly who had enough problems of his own. Without going into the amazing details of the situation, my only option at that point was to leave school and go back to Pittsburgh.

If you were to hear more of the story you would understand that there was no way in hell I was going back to my sister's house. I love her, but that wasn't a home for a pregnant young woman looking to thrive.

I tried out my maternal grandmother's apartment. She kicked me out for leaving a light on that she had forgotten she left on, while watching her early morning QVC. Old people, haha. Plan A didn't work.

I tried my aunt's home. She has a nice four bedroom house where she was living all alone. I didn't know how to tell her that I was pregnant. I was scared of the rejection and had no clue what to say so I didn't say anything. Nope, instead I left my positive pregnancy test out with her belongings which I knew she'd see before I woke up the next morning. I was praying she would find it and help me like I believed my mother would have done. That's what you do after your sister passes. You help her child as though she was your own. I woke up the following day to her telling me that her big beautiful home, that we lived in alone, was too small for the both of us, and that she needed her space. Plan B didn't work.

I tried my mentor's house from my youth ministry program. I guess youth ministry and not being married to your child's father don't go hand in hand. The only way Rondell could spend time in town with me was at a hotel. Being young, pregnant, and broke didn't leave space for a hotel in the budget. You guessed it. Plan C didn't work.

I landed myself at my best friend's mother's house, and that turned out to be the largest blessing I had received in a long time. Over the past 20 years, I have since grown to call her my mother, my godmother, or whatever you want to call her. But she's become my earthly mother and I'm eternally grateful to finally have someone who is still around who loves me as her own.

She wasn't there to fix me either. My daughter, Imani, was born in 2001. She was beautiful. Perfect! All 5 pounds 9 ounces of her melted my heart and drove me to mature into a mother. There was nothing I wouldn't do to try to provide for her. I guess that's what all new mothers say and trust me, it was true.

I had worked things out with her father when we were about 2 months pregnant and we had made the decision that we'd raise her as a family. When she turned just under 5 months old, we did what some broke parents do who want the best life for their baby and there's nothing left to offer at home. We went away to the Army. Something inside of me just wouldn't let me stick around to follow the path that I had learned over the years. I didn't want the typical 9 to 5. I didn't want her growing up on the same streets that I had seen drown many people into it's core. I wasn't moving back to North Philly where Rondell was from because he didn't even want to move there. So, we enlisted and shipped right off.

We sacrificed and left her for a year while we found our footing. I was blessed to have a cousin who nurtured and loved her in ways that I don't believe I was mentally capable of doing at the time. I had my own mommy issues and those were not what my daughter deserved.

While in the military we moved to Germany where we had our second child, Rondell, in 2002. He was a beautiful 6 pound 12 ounce boy with the cutest 2 dimples. Our daughter Imani was there with us in Germany in time for the birth so our family was whole and for once, in a stable home. Our newest addition was there because we both had lacked a stable family back home and we wanted to grow one out of love.

We were happy. Bills were paid (by the Army), food was always on the table, and the medical facility was a walk away. I know a lot of people knock the military. They say we don't get paid enough for what we do. But, when you're coming from nothing and now everything was taken care of, that knowledge of the dark brought light to every small detail. We had found our bliss on Ft. Bliss.

We soon moved to El Paso, Texas. By that time I had separated from the Army myself and had become a stay at home mother, while I was taking the crash course of learning what a mother even was. First time parents go into this situation of parenthood thinking that we know what we're doing because we've seen it done. We've either had mothers of our own or we've seen them in other's homes or on television. Many try to become the person that we wanted to have when we were younger that never truly existed outside of our mind's eye. So we think, "that's what I'm going to give my kids," and on many occasions we fail. This mothering shit is not easy, to say the least. However, I kept doing it.

By the time we left Texas in 2006 we had become parents of 3 beautiful souls. My second daughter was now 2 months old. Our family was complete. So rightfully, we named her Trinity. She was my completion to my 3 children with a house, two failed dogs that wound up in a humane society because having a dog adds the responsibility of a COMPLETE child to your life, and a couple of cats that my husband hated.

With both of us being from the city suffering from a massive lack of financial education, the money that we were making came into one pocket and quickly went directly out of the other. We had not learned to save and we hadn't learned to invest, at the time. We just knew that we were finally able to give ourselves and our kids the things that we never had. And this required a little more income than we were making, mostly with our home being a one income home with 3.5 kids including myself.

We started digging ourselves into debt so there was no looking back or getting out. The comfortability of the military was to be our home until they were done with us.

We were blessed to move to our next duty station which was in Japan. It was beautiful. I had finally made it to my first beach on an actual island and was blessed to call this oasis "home" for the next 3 years. For the first time in my life I was becoming a part of a community of ladies who were becoming my sisters. I thought I had it together. I was on the right path.

On the inside I was totally broken. Wounds that are not healed properly will eat away at you until they become infections. I was still that young girl who had never taken time to heal. While he was at work, I was at home wishing I had a break on so many days. I had gone from high school to international mother of 3 in the blink of an eye and lost all focus on developing past the girl who had walked out of Peabody High School.

On many days, following in my father's footsteps of escaping, everything made more sense by noon. I was a six pack in and just fuzzy enough to go about my day without losing my mind to the smallest things. He had taught me to drink the pain away. He never allowed me to see his healing so I did not even know that was an option. I believed that the crap that was on the inside was supposed to stay on the inside because life was in the now and that was all that mattered. That was such garbage and I was not the only one sitting in it.

My kids had friends but they didn't have me. Meanwhile, all I ever wanted was for my husband to come home and take care of all of us. With my scars lingering behind every closed eye, I needed an outlet. I enrolled back in school but was lovingly reminded that I didn't need to go if I didn't want to. So I didn't. I enrolled my daughter in childcare 2 days a week so I could take time off and focus on me but was reminded that our bills, which were minute and horribly managed, were larger than my need for free time. She quickly got pulled out until she started school. I had no clue what I was doing and with their father's focus on development in the military, I was often left alone to nurture myself.

He was a great love. He tried to shower us with love in his known way. But, he wasn't the father figure I was looking for and to this day I thank God for that. He was meant to be a lifelong friend and I'm grateful for that friendship. Had that not existed, my next decision could have broken most relationships to no return. Thankfully, it did not.

By the time 2008 hit I was tired of being locked in and not receiving the help I required. This, of course, was my fault because I was still looking externally. I went back to the theater which was my normal escape mechanism. The stage had always taken me away from reality. I had acted in the theater in Germany performing in "Cinderella" as an evil step sister and as Mazeppa who liked to "bump it like a trumpet" in

"Gypsy".

Now, while in Okinawa, Japan, I joined a program called POPS. The Pacific Okinawa Players. It was so refreshing to be back behind the curtains on stage. I was able to produce that façade again and present happiness to the world. 2 shows in and I was starting to feel great. I finally got to do the show "Ragtime" which I had seen on Broadway my junior year in high school. Then we jumped right into "Nuncrackers" which is a hilarious musical about a disarrayed convent during the holiday season.

My husband worked all of the time pushing towards a much needed and deserved promotion, which I respect him for now. He's currently a First Sergeant serving in Iraq with his name on the list for earning Sergeant Major, which is the top rank that the Army, offers for his efforts.

The theater in Okinawa is where I found the beginning of my next journey. While he was serving I was at home mentally melting into my feelings and the escape to theater introduced me to a young lady who, at the time, helped me. She actually listened to me. She encouraged me to put one of my children in daycare two days a week, reminding me that I had to take time for myself. She was completely taken aback when I told her I had enrolled in college and never went because I was "comfortable sitting at home because my husband was taking care of us so." I didn't need to go back to school. She reminded me that I was better than that and that I deserve to control my own world. I guess she said the perfect things that all smooth people say in order to get what they want. Those things alone aren't the reasons I left my husband.

Yup, you read that right, I left him. In my own defense, my leaving was necessary. It was the only way I would heal myself.

He let me leave with no fight, which broke my already damaged heart. I saw, in him, yet another person who didn't want me the way I needed him to. I gave myself many excuses for why I left. Many of them I attempted to blame on him. He had taken me away and left me alone on an island, was the main one.

In reality I left because the person that I was now seeing showed me that she was broken as well. On many occasions those things that we should be aware of, those red flags, popped up. And they popped up often and were MASSIVE! In so many ways, the fear of me "letting" someone else lose their life crippled me into thinking I needed to be there to catch her.

You see, there is something that I later learned in marriage counseling and truthfully in life with her. I learned to use the "I's" instead of the "You's" because the "You's" will never help you change the only thing that you can change which is the "I." Once again, this is another person who's own story is so tangled that it needs to be written out by another author for it's delicacy. However, the young girl that had made it through the streets of Pittsburgh thought that I could help her. And why not? She was helping me. I had finally found a place of being of use while exploring new boundaries and in that, I thought, I had found my joy.

Moral of the story, never join theater. HAHAHAAA, I'm joking, I'm joking. Get your panties out of a bunch you thespians reading this. I still love the stage.

My lovely Earth Mother Celeste

1SG Clement (center)-Ft. Hood, Tx-(photographer- Alberto Chapaflores)

Part ii- Post POPS, in more than one way

(Sue me, I'm a mom who tells bad dad jokes. Blame Mike)

-I'm going to take a quick pause here to address a few readers. I realize that many people may pick a good book due to the title, the author, the cover, or even word of mouth. There's always a select group who read a book to get the juicy details for their own self pleasure, or in layman's terms, being nosy. If that's your motivation, I pray you keep reading for possible healing past this point. HOWEVER, your thirst won't be quenched here. As you've noticed, the unfortunate stories that I've shared here in detail, are all of those that are dead and gone. Those that most don't remember anyway. I'm not here to destroy the reputation of anyone because that has never been a goal in my life. So, don't expect your next post or call to be about "that thing you just read about so-n-so in Yo's book. For all intents and purposes, that's not the reason I wrote this so put your notebooks away. I do thank you, however, for taking time to read the stories of my life because we all have an origin that leads to this very moment. I pray this allows you to continue on to your next point in peace. I wish you well.-

* * *

My loves Rondell, Imani, Trinity, and I

Closing out 2009, I moved back to my hometown believing that Pittsburgh was the only place I could make it without my ex husband. I had to have a place where I had family and knew how to get to a local hospital in case of an emergency. I was, again, looking for a support system or a safety net in case I failed.

Man, I wish I would have paid attention to those red flags before I left Japan. HOWEVER, this is the time in life where I embraced my motto of "Everything happens for a reason." EVERYTHING happens for a reason. Even when the red flags look like a bright shining object luring me in, that fact still stands.

After 8 years of service as a soldier, reservist, and then an Army spouse, I again became a "civilian." That's what military folk are taught to call people who never served before or who are not currently serving in the military. Even our civilian clothes were called "civvies".

While serving in the Army I graduated from Advanced Individual Training at the top of my class as the Distinguished Honor Graduate. I had proven something to myself that I did not know I could actually do. Your girl was actually a little smart when she put her mind to it. That was my first instance of personal achievement. That gave me an initial sense of self worth.

Now at 28 years old, when I landed back where I had left off at 20 years of age, I went to Dental Assisting school and graduated with straight A's. I got the job that most of the class had wanted at the Dental School. I did my internship with the students of the University Of Pittsburgh Dental School and then went on to be hired in the private practice where the school's instructors saw their private patients. I quickly realized that I was actually good at this thing called life when I applied myself.

On the home front, however life wasn't all that I expected it to be cracked up to be. The honeymoon stayed on the island washed away with the waves.

Over the next six years in that pseudo family composed of myself, my 3 children, and my wife I took on the role of the help. I believed that my helping another would truly help me find myself. My purpose would somehow be fulfilled. Through the disarray at home I came up with the theory that you cannot continue to leave a pot of boiling water on a stove. If you boil water without replenishing the water in the pot for too long the water will evaporate. Then you're left with a smoldering burned pot. Eventually that pretty pot will wind up learning to get off of the stove and hop its own self in the sink or melt to it's death.

As the owner and protector of that pot you have to fill it. You'd have to occasionally turn the heat off, let it cool down a little, wash it, let it sit, refill it, and only then will that trusty pot boil for you for eternity.

The waves that I faced over those six years allowed me to become the pot that hopped off of the stove on her own. Dental assisting was great but one year in I decided I needed more. I went to college and graduated with a Bachelors in Health Science because, after realizing that I had lived a life that needed to heal from many pains, I wanted to help other people. People who get screwed tend to want to help people. I also spent many days at home trying to help a situation that was very reflective of me sitting on the stove being that pot that was boiling with no water, burning, not being refilled. Through the ups and downs, I sat on that stove. Through stories that I can't repeat, I sat on that stove.

It's eye opening to me as I write this, I sit here at 39 years old wanting to share a story with you that still draws fear to my core. I would love to go into chapters with you like I did before about how this happened or that happened. However, after everything I had faced leading up to that failed marriage these 6 years were the scariest by far. The trauma my children and I were introduced to... the manipulation... the twisted lies that were put out to the world so eloquently that I lost more people than I gained in my life... the fights that my children heard as they drifted off at night... the marks that I hid for years... the wired teeth I had to have fixed, blaming them on a cousin to protect the blacked out predator.

Those stories aren't ready to come out yet. Those stories are still a part of my healing process caked on to the bottom of my pot. Don't burn your pot, good people.

On January 6th 2013, our family introduced the youngest Rodriguez to our home. My wife birthed her and I didn't adopt her because deep in my soul she was already my daughter. We gave her a name after her grandfather, my father, Michael Victor Rodriguez, whose birthday was the following day, January 7th. It was an honor after not carrying her for her to carry our family name. He once told me as a young girl to never lose his family name. He would say "its our tradition to keep our family's name alive." and with him having no sons and my oldest children carrying their father's last name, I was finally blessed to satisfy the tradition.

She was a part of me. I stayed up long nights with her. I attended all Dr. appointments. I taught her mother how to breastfeed. As a mother, the list goes on and on. It was a blessing because after raising my own 3 children by trial and error I was able to help a young woman mold herself into a mother. All of this happening in the midst of a turmoil my wife was facing internally. I loved every minute of being a mother to my baby in that situation. But by 2016, I was realizing the gut sinking reality that this perfect little girl might not be in my home as my daughter forever.

Her mother and I had already failed. We had truthfully failed before we conceived her. She'd quickly tell you that I never wanted another baby. In reality, I knew we weren't ready for that journey together from jump. I had been warned in Okinawa that the day would come when she'd want to have a child and to be aware of the things that would be attached to it all. By this point into her and my story, my pot was scorched and starting to melt. The last year of living in that house that was no longer a home was when I finally noticed that my children couldn't take the smell of the burn any longer.

Honestly, I wish I could let you know more about the memories that still haunt us. Maybe my sharing would bring back the family that believed the lies they heard and still hear until this day from her. On the other hand, maybe it would also let the dogs off of the leash that I've been holding so tightly to protect the one who hurt me. The few who knew the truth, I begged to never do any harm in my name. I don't want that so the stories are irrelevant.

Instead, I hold the truth of those dark days in my mind, locked in a vault to be forgotten in time. I've decided that instead of blaming her, I blame me for not leaving sooner. For allowing myself to stay where, on many occasions, I feared for my life. I blame myself for thinking I was in any way capable of helping someone that damaged while I was the one who needed to be saved. While my children learned what true mental illness looks like. I blame me for staying.

Not long after my youngest daughter was born my wife and I had started hanging out with new people together and separately. I learned about some new drinks. Who would have thought that people actually mix a shot of brown liquor and a glass of wine that was already too harsh for many to handle and call this the drink of choice. But, I joined in. I thought it was cool. The friends and the drinks let me disappear from the melting pot. The new associates gave me the courage to participate in dangerous acts like drinking and driving. The community gave me nights and weekends away, which I had not experienced since being a teenager, to party and listen to music. They showed me a blessing and a curse. I was able to learn new forms of escape. I was able to have my new reality and find comfort in bottles, bodies, music, and dark bedrooms that didn't belong to me. I was even able to hide from my wife at times and the children who's eyes I didn't want to see me failing.

Their mother was failing in front of them. She was becoming a functional alcoholic and was quickly spiraling to a point of no return. Living in this home where they were introduced to mental health issues like bipolar disorder, and borderline personality disorder was never the home that I wanted to give them. Before this they had already seen enough so adding that life in to their experience was pushing past forgiveness. And all I felt I could do was stand back and watch. While I was in my personal low, my depression was at an epic high. I would lay in bed and hold my breath and imagine, that for an instant, I was gone. Then I'd remember that pain I faced being an orphan and take another breath pushing the suicidal thoughts to the corner with the memories. I didn't want my children to have that pain and have to face this fucked up world alone.

We started to fail financially. Even though I was working full time as a caseworker for the state and working some weekends as a Dental Assistant to try to make ends meet, the mortgage wasn't being paid on time. It became insanity doing the same thing over and over again expecting it to work the next month. I believe the path to my bankruptcy came with the underlying fear of actually paying those bills on time and being stuck in that home, on that stove, in that marriage, forever.

Don't get me wrong, I always knew I wanted the house. It was 5,000 sq. feet with 5 bedrooms and 4.5 bathrooms; an inground 8 foot pool; an 8 person jacuzzi; an elevator; a library; 3 fire places; an outdoor cabana; a 15 car parking deck; a wrap around enclosed porch; almost an acre of back, side, and front yard; a steam room; and in floor jacuzzi in my bathroom. All of that and I still needed out of the darkness surrounding me and my children. To me it was simply a house and self sabotage became a method that was working to help me rid us of it.

I prayed on many days that the blood family that I came home to back in 2009 would reach out and help us. Reach my children, reach me, hold us, and give us the help that we so desperately needed. That they would step up and be the foundation that we were lacking from my mother and father. But, they never came. I never shared with them the truth of what was happening to us behind those closed doors so they possibly did not know how alone I was. The form of help they would have given had they heard the stories would have given more heart ache in the long run so it was best kept in my journals.

I kept telling myself I was a good person who deserved more, not realizing that what you deserve isn't what comes from other people. It's from what you give yourself. I was looking outward to be rescued when all along I needed to search deeper within.

My job as a caseworker ended one rainy day (that sounds cheesy but it's true) as I had already decided that I wanted to be an entrepreneur for the rest of my life and never look back. I just never knew when to make the move. After using all of my leave and after experiencing how a Familial Medical Leave of Absence would not pay the bill, my income added to my having to leave my job.

In April of 2017, I walked into my office for the last time, covered in bruises and scratches that were my excuse for why I was late once again. However, this time I wasn't prepared to hide them. I showed up in jeans, a T-shirt, and a hoodie on my head when our required uniform for work was business casual. The scars in my heart were why my work was not being completed, because I couldn't focus on the subject at hand. I was constantly focused on how to make home make sense. Everything was suffering.

The night before had broken me. The sights I saw in my bathroom shattered any focus I had on my being the one who who could be help. Instead, I only saw the person inside of my wife that was blocking her from seeing that she could be helped. That's when I went from wanting to save my friend to hating the person within her that wouldn't allow her to save herself. She was trapped and in her eyes that night, I had finally seen her captor.

I tried to go to me desk and instantly realized that I couldn't hide any longer. I sat with my supervisor and my manager behind closed doors and finally called a helpline. I didn't lie that day about where the visible scratches on my neck had come from as I did when they were seen back in Dental Assisting school. Back then I was still perfecting a lie and told a friend they were from rough sex. I was still protecting someone at that time. In this office, after the very long past 24 hours, I was finally searching for help to get me out of this melting situation. The late nights of my children hearing the screams in the house had to end. I called that line and begged but that help never came the way I needed it to. And my 2 weeks notice landed on my manager's desk shortly after.

* * *

Part iii- Hope...

In every sad story there's a moment when, if the main character notices it and reacts differently, the story could change and do a complete 180 turnaround.

My moment occurred a short time later in the back of a police car handcuffed and heading to the Allegheny County Jail (ACJ).

Have you ever watched one of those shows where they tell a story of a person who had a complete mental break and the next thing they know they're sitting with blood on their hands and have no clue where it came from? Well, my story wasn't bloody, thank God, but, waking up to the cops knocking and then throwing me into their car was a big ass wake -me-up and I'm grateful that in that second I listened.

For the year prior to this cold dark ride to the Penn Hills precinct and the next ride after the transfer of officers to be delivered to ACJ, I had been quickly partying and melting my life away. I mean, drinking was my new norm which I had always wanted to avoid after life with my father. That combined with freedom of sex, mind you, I was 35 years old and at one of my sexual peaks, and my need to run away all quickly had me playing chicken with a midlife crisis.

I had said for weeks in advance that I felt "off". That I was losing love and that I could not take it any longer. I begged for help. I begged to be taken off of that stove OFTEN. Until being pushed. Until seeing blood the night before I quit my job, in places where it shouldn't have been, and no longer knowing how to help my wife save herself from herself, I was officially done.

In that moment in that car with no padding on the seats I realized my kids had no mother. My then, 16 year old daughter was at home, nurturing all 3 of my crying babies who had watched me be cuffed and taken away. I had lost all focus on them and was trying to free my partner. The fight had started over money again and quickly led to me having to protect my child who was there trying to protect me.

To top it all off, the one person who I had followed down that dark wet rat hole was about to be there with them to whisper "I got you kids. Everything will be alright." Even though I fought that night to protect my oldest daughter from harms way, I was still losing them. Not only that, they were losing me. Had I continued on the path that we were on in that home, they too would have become her empty burning pots and I couldn't let that happen. They would think of me and write a book one day about my weakness that I wouldn't be proud to read if I stayed in that dot of darkness. The stories I hear to this day about things they encountered while I wasn't around make me grateful for that story ending.

If not for me, at least for them, I needed saved! Crazy thing is when you believe you need to be saved, you have given way to the possibility that you actually could be saved. And THAT'S when hope calls. In that instant I listened!

I instantly realized that sitting overnight in that jail on a brick slab where the lights never went out was for other women who were comfortable in that environment. This situation was for the ones in the room with me laughing because they had been in there so many times they knew the officers and the routine. They showed me that I wasn't cut out for that life. I wasn't meant to fail. I wasn't meant to let others drag me under. And I was no longer making excuses for others determining where my life was headed. I was in charge of me! I decided that my RE-actions were still the actions that I chose. My staying around was MY choice. My children deserved better than that.

I was blessed as that next morning the judge saw my heart instead of my actions and let me go with no bail. I stood in front of a judge on a computer screen in front of a room full of people from all over my city who watched. Not knowing me, not knowing my story, not knowing where I was coming from they sat and watched me be judged for MY actions. That was the last place I ever want to return to. For as quickly as that actual moment went by, I felt like hours went by with all of their eyes on me. I had to make an instant decision. I had to look within. And in whatever moment you are in on your journey, you can decide too.

When I walked out of ACJ that day I weighed 134 pounds. A year before I weighed 155 pounds. I measure five' nine" and at my normal weight I was already a thin girl. The life of drinking more than I ate was failing me. Depression had led me to hospital visits for things that the doctor could not find a diagnosis for. Endoscopies and colonoscopies to see why I couldn't eat let alone move my bowels became a norm. Visits to the neurologists to find out why my vision would go blurry and my arms would go numb were a regular. I'd have talks with the dietician to help me gain weight that was deteriorating away. Trips to the cardiologist because my heart would race at 245 beats per minute for almost an hour at time to leave diagnosed with a broken heart was the end game. Stress was killing me. I thought back to my mom and my father who were gone then, thought of my children. I couldn't let my children lose me. I had to reach me.

When I saw the sun that morning leaving ACJ I decided to live. You see, that's the big thing you have to do on this journey to wherever you are going. We each have a story! We each have a dark mark that we know of that is supposed to be a part of this light that we are living. However, without the decision to learn from those marks the pathway into the black hole continues until it becomes a vortex that's unescapable. We blame others to escape our obligation to help ourselves. We look for help to blame people for not helping us properly.

We say things like "but if he wouldn't have," "if my mother wouldn't have," "YOU DON'T KNOW MY CHILDHOOD!" And it's flat out BULLSHIT! Those people have their own screwed up things floating around in their own screwed up heads that they are trying to fix. If the life we are living isn't the life that we want we have to look inside. We have to decide that it's time to win. If not, we never will!

MommyYo (me) teaching MyBunk (my baby Rodriguez) to walk down the aisle as the perfect flower girl for a friend's wedding-2016

Part iv- No one, ABSOLUTELY NO ONE, Can Save You

It may sound too black and white, but it's TRUE. I've heard it all. My pastor, my mentor, and even people with the audacity to place the load and blame on God. Look, it's up to NO ONE to save you! If you are a religious being, God may show you the way and guide or hold you through the difficult times. But God doesn't stop you from the negative crap that you are doing to sabotage His/Her work. And in the instant that your wrong doing turns to something bad in your life people revert straight to "Father why have you forsaken me?" How unfair is that??? It was YOU! It was ME!

OK, the decision to win doesn't automatically mean that life will be great. There's a guarantee that time and time again after that decision your actions will still lead to failure. It's the natural ebb and flow of growth and learning.

You see, at this point in my journey, my then wife and daughter had moved out of our joint home. My older children and I were loving each other again and becoming more trusting of each other. I believe they were just old enough to have compassion for me. I was trusting them to allow me to heal and they were trusting me to not fail or leave and give up. Once they gave me that trust I knew that if I had broken it one more time there was no getting it back. I had to take the blame for that and not allow it to happen.

Even though I had been in my industry for some years now, this was when I actually started pursuing my journey to becoming an entrepreneur. I know right? We're talking about mental healing here. But you see this was major for me because my taking charge of my complete development and freedom was equal to me taking charge of my life, mentally. I was also being introduced to people who knew that the path to this success started with your own mental health.

I had a mentor who knew some of the things I faced. When he saw that I wasn't pushing forward in life in the way that I said that I wanted to, he would call me and say "Yo, what are you reading?" It's true what they say, every great leader is a great reader. I had heard it many times before and it went in one ear and out of the other. This time, after he asked me for the 10th time, I finally had an answer. I told him "nothing." Teachers in school have you read to grow. But I had graduated from school and not one of the books I had read since then was about personal development. How did I expect to grow from what I didn't know? So, I decided to listen. He said I needed to fix myself. I needed to follow the path that was already laid out by many people before me that taught people how to heal. So, with hesitation I became a purposeful reader. Now mind you, I was a reader before this. I read sci-fi, erotica, and many other genres. But you know, what you put in is what comes out. I needed to put out self healing. I needed to eat it for breakfast, lunch, and dinner. Instead, what I was reading had me thinking of, well, I'll leave that up to your own imagination.

Healing wasn't quick. I still had my occasional flings with what some people call "kut" buddies, who fulfilled some of my physical needs but none of my mental needs. I had an amazing friend who wanted to nurture my soul who I never got emotionally close to because she was a good person and there's no way I could damage one of those while I was in this state (self awareness saves friendships). I had a few others, here and there, who were fillers on lonely nights. On the inside, all I had was me. I had to face my own demons. I had to look at myself in the mirror just as you do every single day.

I look back and remember one of the conversations that I had with my ex wife, and I use the word conversation very loosely. But in that conversation she asked me "What the f*ck do you want Yolanda?" And I screamed "I want someone who will laugh with me. I want someone who would hold me while I cry without flipping the script so that shortly after I was holding them instead. I want someone who will allow me to be silly without thinking I was being childish or rolling their eyes at me. I want someone who would understand that at times I don't remember everything, be it due to either mental damage I had, or blocking out reality because of fear of what I had to face. I want someone who can smile and light up a room and NOT just for the other girl across the room. I want someone who would never EVER scream and holler at me. I want someone who would never cheat on me. Someone who would never abuse me. Someone WITHOUT mental disorders that I didn't feel like I had to take care of. I want someone who didn't show the world their amazing side after using me as their doormat while walking out of the house. I want someone who loved me just for me and allowed me to go through my healing process without giving me more burden. Because I felt weak, I want someone who reminds me I was strong. I want a home that I love to come home to everyday. I want bills paid. I want my children to love me again. I want it all!" I screamed that to the universe and the heavens or anything that would listen. After reading the book "The Law of Attraction" all that I could do was scream it in belief that I would be heard.

As my words left my lips I realized that if I didn't improve myself that person that I had just asked for would leave quicker than I could even learn her last name. So, I started some self work. That hope was in my heart and if I even remotely imagined that this amazing made up person existed, I didn't want that opportunity to arise when I wasn't prepared. I'd rather be prepared and if they never came at least I'd know that I was enough and ready.

I stopped sleeping around. I stopped drinking every day. And I stopped laying in bed on the days when I had no work just melting my story into oblivion. After hearing the answer that I gave her I had to stop and think for a minute. What was I bringing to the table? I had asked for some pretty amazing shit from a person and still laid in bed at night crying to myself without fixing me. Often staring at a half empty glass of wine. If that person walked into my front door they'd be walking out of the door within no time and I'd be the one who would have held it open for them and pushed them out.

I had to take a leap. I had to take a step for myself and I knew I would fail multiple times. Still, I had to fail forward, no matter what.

All of the people that had been around my life during that last year of my marriage were there for their own reason but none of them to save me. Literally no one can save you. No one. People can love your body. They can even lust for you day in and out. The touches you feel may feel great in the moment. Your mind goes places where your abuse, neglect, drugs, alcohol, and laziness can't go. They may buy you a new house or a shiny car that can help you feel secure. They can assure you financially that your children will eat every single day and that the lights will never go out on those nights when you can't sleep for hours because of the memories. Arms can hold you at night and rock you back to sleep after the nightmares that reflect your memories. Their words can tell you that things will never go back to the old way. They can tell you to read, exercise, listen to motivational speakers. Others can do literally anything to attempt to help you.

In the end, no matter what, you are alone. When they're rocking you and rubbing your head, letting you know it's all going to be okay or when they're reassuring you that those things are long gone and in the past, you are still alone. Only you are in your head, only you see the images that play on automatic replay in your mind's eye. These lonely, scary, dark images that encourage you to stay in bed for days saying "I'm sorry, I'm just not feeling good today.", these memories that make, even you, start to question how many times a person could say "sorry" in any given hour.

Someone says to you "The batteries in a remote just died." and you respond with, "I'm sorry, I must have..." Knowing good and damn well all that someone has to do is go to the drawer or run to the store and get new batteries. Yet, you/WE revert to "I'm sorry."

Someone says "The water bottles aren't cold yet." and you say "I'm sorry, maybe I must have..." instead of simply getting a cup of ice, or God forbid just agreeing and saying "Yeah, you're right. The water isn't cold enough, yet. Maybe it needs to stay in the fridge a little longer." Of all of the things that can be said, the "damaged ones" tend to revert back to the good old "I'm sorry." for all of them. A phrase that we have trained ourselves to use so often because we want the bullshit to stop. The damage is within and no one lurks in there except for you and you alone.

"I'm sorry" isn't the only sign of a mentally abused person either. There's many other things that I found myself doing that just did not seem right for a healthy individual. I stopped standing in front of a mirror completely undressed. I didn't want to see that I hadn't worked out in a long time or that some of the bumps and bruises on my body weren't from other people. Some were simply from me blindly banging into things with my lack of mental focus. I didn't want to face my intentionally or unintentionally having cuts and scratches on my wrist. I didn't want to see the abs that I once had now turned into a small beer belly that I had perfected holding in when I was wearing those cute jeans. I didn't want to see the yellow of my teeth that was caused by that coffee that I drank to keep me up or the lack of hygiene I was allowing myself on a daily basis. I didn't want to see the white fading from my eyes due to lack of sleep or the continuous inebriation. I had asked for someone to want and look at a woman who would not even look at herself. This needed fixed because in the backseat of that cop car I had found hope. Just like I pray you do as well.

I'm sure you're wondering where I'm going with this and how does this have anything to do with the Yin-Yang in the beginning? Are we going to talk about fried chicken or what? No, we're not talking about fried chicken. However, the dark that I went through over the prior 35 years, that led up to that moment gave me knowledge. It gave me awareness of my version of darkness. My dark gave me an appreciation for the positive things that were to come. And like the downs you have faced in your life, it gave me my dot which introduced me to the light.

"Street nights" 2017 with Photographer Mr. Ty Smith of
Blacksmith Digital Images

Chapter 5 Questions- The Blame Game

Who do you charge with not fixing the you that you sit with today? Trust me we all blame someone. They walked into your life, you thought they would be the end to the inner trauma, and yet, you still hear your OWN words reminding you otherwise. The cries inside still ring out to you. Who walked out the door and never returned. They may be the one that you call who listens but cannot fix it all. That person might be laying next to you while you are reading this very line. Don't worry, I won't tell them.

You can also add in here why you thought they'd be able to change/help you? What did they have that you were lacking that you believed would be, in some form, your saving grace?

-

-

-

-

-

-

-

What are the bad habits that you have perfected that you KNOW you need to break? The routines or tendencies that you use to drown out the inner noise and you may even, at times, hide from those around you.

-

-

-

-

-

-

-

-

-

-

-

-

What are these practices holding you back from achieving?
ex: "If I stopped hitting that snooze button I could...."

-

-

-

-

-

-

-

-

-

-

-

-

Chapter 6- You Decide!

Part i- You WILL Fail, But Get Back Up

*J*ust as no two stories read the same, no two healings are the same, either. I'm very aware that you have been through some things that I can not start to imagine. In many instances those events were more traumatic than this story that you are currently reading. You may actually wish that your life was as easy as mine. I get it! However, even you can heal. You have to! I give you a "you should do this," scenario. What I can tell you is, it is imperative for your physical and mental health that you find what works for you. Heck, find multiple things that work for you and use the same energy that you used to sink into your hole, to your benefit while climbing into your success.

I know you may not have heard this before because as far as I know I just made it up, but listen closely. To fail takes discipline. Believe it or not, it does. After pain, we decide how long, how deeply, and how negatively we live in our pit. The decision to stop hanging with our friends who continue the same negative habits. To say over and over and over again how we're going to start working out to get our bodies back in shape starting next Monday with such a stern dedication of going 52 Mondays, but change that vow into a New Year's resolution, and stick to it, takes a lot of discipline. Mostly, if you do that for a couple of years in a row. So, stop fooling yourself into believing you CAN'T. That you don't have what it takes and, for goodness sakes, that you need someone else to get you there.

Yes, being a depressed person takes work. The small white dot in this dark place is that we do learn discipline. We learn it through repeated failures that we allow ourselves to face. To fall into the darkness we actually see that we can be good at something. Even if it is rolling ourselves out of bed and dolling ourselves up when we go out in public so that other people can see us as put together. That takes practice. You got good at something.

Man, I have never used so much makeup in my life as I figuratively did when I was appearing to look like a competent human being for those 7 years. All while my insides cried for my bed. Because I needed a good nap all of the time.

This is what you have to use as fuel. Beginning the path to finding or even re-finding ourselves is a process of first deciding where we're going and then learning the positive disciplines to get you there.

After all of the ups and downs in my story, I found myself never wanting to work for anyone again. It was probably due to the fact that I did not want to wake up on schedule, but still generate enough money to feed my family, and myself.

It's interesting that our eating is one of the first things we might be willing to sacrifice when we're lost and have to feed others.

In 2016, I partnered with some people from Ohio who were following simple disciplines to get that time and financial freedom that I was praying for.

Okay, don't put the book down. I'm not trying to have you join my business or follow my method. I'm simply sharing my story with you. Cool? Cool.

In my first year with this company, I was blessed to hear multiple testimonials from men and women. All of them had come from their own pits in their respective lives. The one thing they all had in common was that over the past few years they had made a decision to stop making excuses and win. And when I say win, I mean WIN BIG. They were tired of the normal mundane acceptance of where they were and now had the freedom of time as well as financial freedom that I was looking for.

Now, don't get me wrong. I'm not all of the sudden saying that if you have money, you'll be free. That couldn't be farther from the truth. What I did realize was that along my path, one of the main things that I had lacked was time with my children due to working hours chasing the dollar when I wasn't stuck in my own mind. Another thing I was lacking was the finances to give them the home and life that I wanted to provide for them without a second parent in the home. What I heard in those testimonials was a means to solving some of my basic problems. I saw a way to eliminate the need for another person to enter my children's lives for the purpose of helping to pay the bills or give them attention. I saw a life with my children. And the one thing that each of those people had was discipline.

I mean, they embodied it to the max. They had decided and STUCK TO THEIR PLAN.

Where I'm from, if you wanted "freedom" for you and your family you did the normal thing. You got your diploma from high school and you went to college and got a degree. Then, you climbed the ladder in a job that you dread in order to get to 60K or so a year. It didn't take much perfection or decision. It was, do what the bosses tell me, skate by, still do what I do at home, and pray my way to the top.

But then, while on this new journey, I met a person who between him and his wife started their journey with only $134, living in the basement of their mother's home and within four years time were making a six to seven figure income. I met a person who went from being a city bus driver making 30K annually, driving people who would threaten to, and at times, spit on him. Within a few years time he was retired and forever living the life that most of us dream about. I also met a woman who would take her children to school early every day and pick them up after 6pm, cook for them, wash them, and put them to bed only to do the same routine the next day. The other mothers at the daycare that she picked them up from would mock her saying "oh wow, you're always out with this little company while we're spending more time with our children in the evenings. You're wasting your time and neglecting them to follow a false dream. You're not getting anywhere."

She turned things around a year later. When the other mothers' children all had a project on pyramids, the mothers did their research in a book. My friend was able to take her children to the great pyramids.

I met people who had mastered positive discipline and found a way out of the situations that they were once in. And I needed a way out of mine and I needed it quickly.

I learned a few things after starting this business. The first thing I learned was that I was a mess, like, a pure and complete utter mess. I'm grateful that I learned it though because the man who thinks they know it all, never learns, and I had a lot to learn.

The second thing that I learned was that no one trusts a person who has proven they don't even trust themselves. I had tools in front of me to "succeed" yet I didn't believe in myself enough to follow the disciplines and actually get there. People literally handed me the keys and blueprint to financial freedom, to my utilities never being turned off due to lack of payment again, and I didn't trust myself enough to follow them. I now believe that I didn't believe that I could. THEY had won. That didn't mean that I could win. I needed to learn to trust myself before I could go any further. I needed to become a student of those around me and to myself. It's very true that no one is here to save you. Yet, there are people who have been where you are in some form and they've made it out. If they can make it out, so can you. And I wanted out. So I had to make this work. I had to find my self trust and discipline and do it quickly.

It was a very humbling situation, when I began to meet these people. I for once had a millionaire's phone number locked into my phone, and like every other person in my phone, they never handed me a penny. I wanted to be angry. I wanted to complain and bitch. "If you have it WHY can't you help me? Don't you see that I'm melting?" And then I realized, they're millionaires. They are there for a reason. They didn't get there by receiving handouts. They got there by discipline. And one of the disciplines is they don't hand out money to just everyone because then they would be broke right along with them. Instead, I had to take away the mental wealth that they were offering. They offered their story of self development. No one had done it for them either. They had to dig in to get where they wanted to be.

There was literally NO ONE to help me without me. I had landed flat on my face in the presence of "great." My hand was outreached and I was left to grab it myself. No matter the, so called, caliber of who I was around, all I could take from them was knowledge. The rest was my journey to face.

At times I hit that failing moment on repeat. I would find a way out, give what I claimed to be my all and honestly in those moments that was my all, and I would fail. I'd reach a hand out for a little nudge and it would be left empty. Those are the most trying moments in growth. The ones where you have to realize that simply because you try it doesn't mean you'll make it. Those are the moments when you have to face yourself in the darkness yet again.

* * *

Part ii- Fail Again… Yup, Again

Seeing that I was going to have to fail again was my major reality check. If the people who literally could help me wouldn't help me then they couldn't help me. It still boiled down to me. Your person might be someone who can let you live with them. Your person might be someone who can cover your bills for a while. Your person might be someone who can simply keep the kids more often. It's easy to decide to quit when that reach for help goes unanswered. To feel lonely again or to feel like "what's the point?" but that's when you really have to dig in and remember the reason you're going.

My mentor who always asked me "What are you reading, Yolanda," showed up at my house one day after a rough fight with my ex. He had driven over 2 hours from Ohio to have this moment with me. We drove through my town for about six hours that day. We did a little work. We did a lot of talking. We ate. I cried. And he asked me again "Yolanda, what are you reading?" I wasn't reading anything. After fighting back for whatever made up reason for that year of hearing it from him, I finally had to give in. He along with every successful person I knew, had told me to read. I wasn't doing it yet I claimed to want success. I was being stubborn.

After going to all of these events one book that they recommended, and that I'm now recommending to you, stood out to me. It's called "Start With Why" by Simon Sinek. Some companies will say "why" means What Hurts You. What makes you wake up in the morning, even when you don't want to. What makes you keep going. Some people say "why" means WHY are you doing what you're doing.

All I knew was, after learning my WHY, I realized that if I did not fight for it, they would have their own tragic story to tell in the future. My why was my children's mental health in the future, not just what they thought of me today. My WHY was the woman who had taken on the role of mother to me and grandmother to my children. The one whose home was falling apart and had no one to give back to her what she had given to so many of us young, lost hood kids for years on end. My WHY was remembering how it felt as a young girl to not have parents and knowing that I never wanted my children to face the same feeling. My WHY was wanting to see my grandchildren and for them to have a stable grandmother. My WHY was just wanting to be old one day. Not wanting to be in pain and arthritic, but to be in my later years with silver hair, watching the world evolve while watching my children's lives get to a point where they didn't necessarily need me anymore. I wanted to grow to irrelevance to their daily needs. I guess I had a lot of WHYs. I had to focus on all of them because the things that took me down were big so I needed my WHY to be huge to pull me back up. My mentor also always told me if "your WHY doesn't make you cry you need to dig deeper into your WHY until it does." And man did I ever cry.

I'm sure if you're still reading this book, many of you have had situations where you've faced your life, I mean really looked at it, and all you could do was break out in tears. All you could do in those moments was hug yourself because you felt like no one else was there to hug the true pain within. Well, I was crying myself to sleep every night. I remember when I was a little girl my father used to tell me, "Man Puddin, you've cried so many tears I'm surprised you have any left to come out of your body." Welp, guess what dad, here's another bucket full for ya.

I had to remind myself of those WHYs every single day in order to get my shit together. The fact that no one would ever help me and that it took me 35 years to learn that was a blessing. I had the opportunity to learn many hard lessons in that time. I learned lessons that I don't believe I would have learned at a younger age. There was so much that others couldn't see that I'm sure they couldn't help me with even if they had tried.

This isn't to say that many people in my life hadn't attempted, in their defense. I sought freedom with others through a number of religions. I studied the teachings of a Jehovah's Witness for some time. I even lived as one for months. I later became a Muslim for about six months to a year the year that my father died. I wore a Hijab, celebrated Ramadan, did my morning and night prayers, and I ate no pork. I tried it. I lived as a Christian from the time when I was 11 years old, less the gap for Islam and learning the laws of being a Witness. I was a practicing Christian until I saw my church crumble when I was in Germany due to the the members of the church. Their judgement and constant displays of negativity is a major reason for why I stepped away from the church, temporarily, and reached back to my Christian family when I landed back in PA in 2009. The slap to the face I got upon my return to the church from the ones who claimed to be my friends from childhood, left me to realize that it's not the religion nor the other people that practice it's job to help me. I continued to do a lot of searching. I studied what it was to live like the Buddha. I did that without worshiping him as a God but living in his way. This was a beautiful path compared to most, however, the inner me still wasn't free.

All of these efforts still led me to believe one thing. I still had to do it for myself. No one, not even one particular God or religion could take me away from the pain that was in my soul. Prayer, fasting, dancing, singing, all of it still only hid what was in my mind.

Now again, don't stop reading this just because we're not on the same religious path. Just know that we each have our own path and I know that different people reading this have different religions. I respect your religious decisions in your life as I pray that you respect mine.

In order to grow and release fully, I had to do some things to find myself. After reading the book "Start With Why" which showed me deeply how my WHY would keep me moving, I began to wake up in the morning to do morning meditation.

It wasn't always easy. My brain would run literally everywhere. About 10 seconds into meditating I was usually thinking about a lot of crap. It was never one thing, but most of these thoughts made me forget I was meditating. I kept trying. I listened to the audios on the internet. I learned deep breathing from my solar plexus and from my diaphragm. I continued to meditate until I learned how to feel healing come from my core and work through my spine to start self healing to my body. It took practice, failure, and more practice.

Since graduating with my degree in 2013, I understood how the nervous system helps your body self heal. I got that the things that happen in your mind send signals to your body to behave or respond in a certain way. Just as my mind had nearly killed me through depression, my mind could heal me in my darkest hours. I had used knowledge to study Reiki and to become attuned, yet I had never actively developed the ability to practice Reiki until this time of meditation. I use my morning meditation to focus on my body healing itself one small piece at a time. After all of the visits to the hospital still showing no sign of diagnosis I had accepted that my DISease was giving me dis-ease.

I soon went back to my teachings in Reiki. Readdressing the fact that not everything hurting you physically stemmed from an ailment taught me to release tension, to release anger, to release fear, to release blame, and to release depression. It taught me to start releasing literal heart break that was based on expectation. Expectation that did not need to exist.

I studied crystal work. I mean, I lived with a tiger eye in my presence and on days when I couldn't focus I always had a fluorite within reach to calm the chatter. An amethyst stayed under the corner of my bed to introduce a peaceful love. I tried to find the purpose of every mineral I laid my hands on. Connecting in all ways possible with my surroundings.

I stopped mixing alcohol. No more beer followed by a couple of glasses of wine. No more wine mixed with a couple of shots. Mainly, no more liquor chasing everything that I put into my body. Almost everyone in my family suffered from alcoholism and that would not be me.

All of these "healing" methods together seem like they should have worked and pulled me right out of the pit that I was in, however I was still unable to use discipline in a positive way. I still had the discipline of waking up late and hitting my snooze alarm 2 to 3 times throughout the week. I still had the discipline of a glass of wine before I went to bed which normally led to about three glasses of wine before the night's end.

Those negative disciplines I had developed plus other cracks in my positive discipline led to my occasional failure. Which, at times made me feel like it was time to give up, yet again. I was blessed that I had become a reader because I was reminded every time that I failed that I had to look again at my WHY.

I continued to read. My next eye opener was a book called "Another Shot" by Dave Martin. I learned that if one method was not working, I had to find another. When that method started to work, I was pretty positive I was going to fail again. But I knew I couldn't stop. I had to continue to catch my OWN rebounds in life and get back in the game.

I had to admit to myself that I was not disciplined in my positive acts and I never did exactly what I said I was going to do. Every single time that I tried, I still sabotaged my efforts by using negative discipline and not being true to my commitments to myself.

That's one of the main things I charge you to do. I challenge you to learn to use your discipline for a positive. Because when you sit by yourself in a room and you think of yourself, not the self that others judge you by, not the self that you've been acting like, not the one that you see in the mirror. When you actually sit and think of your talents and your capabilities, you become aware that you can do things that you want to do.

Do you know how to physically turn off an alarm clock and stand up on two feet? Yes. It's not hard to do. However, we don't do it. Do you know how to pick up a glass of water instead of picking up a bottle of wine or liquor or a couple of beers? Yes. But, the beer feels better so we still grab it first. In your mind you know how to walk to the kitchen and get a glass of water. We don't give ourselves that discipline. We fool ourselves into thinking "I can't fight the urges. Hogwash!

I used to write myself a schedule and put it next to my bed. I was going to wake up in the morning, hopefully. I would write my gratitude; I would do my meditation; I would drink a cup of tea; I would read 10 pages of whatever book I was currently reading, and so on and so forth.

That schedule had to be rewritten every... single... procrastinating... week because I never completed the list and instead of changing my actions I would change my list to match my feelings.

This is what we do! We give up on ourselves. We give ourselves huge excuses and that is why that dreadful pain keeps lingering within us. We never put out the "all" that we say we are going to give and we cry when our half assed attempts don't work. As I've told many people in my industry, "It's not your plan that didn't work for you. It was you that didn't work your plan!"

There's truly no real blueprints in this thing. I'm not telling you to follow my schedule because half the time I don't follow my schedule still. I am still a work in progress, who I guess had to sit down and write this book in order to actually see the real me. I have many layers of myself that I'm still trying to pull back in order for the brightness behind each one to truly shine. I fail multiple times at things that I'm working towards. Now that I know I'm capable of success, capable of no longer being depressed, capable of being who I want to be, capable of being who my children deserve to have as a mother, I plan to and I must finish this journey of life successfully. And only I can do that for me. Just as only YOU can do that for you.

One thing that I've learned to do on my journey thus far, by recommendation from those who have been there in their pit and have found success, is to listen to audio motivational speakers online. Along that process, one audio definitely stood out to me and helped me while I was in my failing process. That's something that was said on one of the videos by Will Smith. I know you all know who Will Smith is. "I robot," "Fresh Prince of Bel Air" Will? Jada's husband. Yeah, that guy.

This guy, Will, from Philadelphia, who is now world renowned, started his discipline by building brick by brick and teaches others that you have to "Fail early. Fail often. And fail forward". Stop and think about those words for a minute. A man who appears to never fail tells the world to do it early, often, and forward. Think about it!

.... You didn't think long enough............................
.... There you go..................................

A lot of people think "I won't start until I know exactly how I can do it, whatever 'it' is, that way I won't fail." That's not how it works! You have to fail early. You have to start on day one. Fail on day one, learn from your failure and repeat the action to learn how to do it without failing. Even if it is taking a daily shower, fail at it.

You have to fail often. I learned from some of my mentors that fast is fun and slow hurts. Going through this process quickly brings reaching milestones on the path to your goals and your successes on a daily basis. Opposed to hitting a failure, which you will hit, stopping because you want to complain about it, waiting a few days, and then trying again. It is a lot more fun to fail often because you get to those successful moments faster. What happens when you take those breaks in the middle to mourn for yourself and cry about how you didn't succeed? You allow yourself time to wonder if you can find success the next time. It hurts to do it with these breaks, so you have to learn to fail often. You have to get up off of your butt and like the old saying goes, get back on the horse. This gives you another opportunity to learn from where you left off without missing the lesson due to your wallowing.

The amazing thing about following those the two habits of failing early and failing often, is the more often you fail and learn from each failure and the more you learn to fail forward automatically it becomes a habit to learn from each mistake. You don't wait until you're too old to enjoy the fruits of your labor. You're in continuous movement towards your peace of mind. You GET THERE. And you get closer to your "there" with each and every failure. Even if getting better means to fall flat on your face harder you hop back up with more ease, more knowledge of what NOT to do, and more determination than the prior time.

I've tried to write this book for about the last 15 years in different ways. At one point it was solely a memoir, but no one wants to sit and read about my story. It's a page turner but it's simply my story. I've started it as an erotica. Believe it or not, that was a really good variation. However, it wasn't right for my goal so, that's literally sitting in an old computer in a landfill in Pittsburgh. I ignored my writing goal for a 3 year period of time. Well, that went nowhere fast, haha MAN! I'm corny. Yeah, I know. It's cool. WHEW!

Finally, I decided to just write. I had no clue where it was going or where it would end. I just knew that I had to do SOMETHING or it would, in time, be buried with me when I left this body. I wasn't ready when I started, however I kept trying. Each time that I started the process, I learned more. I added on more knowledge that gave me a fall forward. Now I find myself with the story on paper and released from my mind. I finished this book because I failed forward. It took me page by page and failure by failure to actually know where I was even going. Typos, grammatical errors, horrible cover decisions, and a formatting process that, well, completely sucked. All of it was a lesson forward.

The same stood with my failures in my daily life. I had attempted to stop drinking multiple times. The first attempt went great. As great as it could go until the kids saw me fall to another one of my low points and land on a bottle. The trust that I had started to gain with them went out the window. I stuck to drinking a while longer in my own self pity until I realized this wasn't helping our relationship. I was stalling the inevitable next failure instead of learning from it. When I went back to not drinking and actually nurturing myself again on a regular, the trust started to rekindle. They stayed around me more. The more time I put in to being sober and focusing on healing, was my learning to fail forward. I had to do it quickly though because if not, I would have lost their trust and with trust gone that would have been an entire new mountain I would have had to climb.

Whatever your healing journey is, I recommend listening to motivational audios along the way. I'm very grateful that I listened to that one because it's that fail early, often, and forward that gains you momentum. If I hadn't taken the time to listen to those various motivators, I never would have caught that message. That may not be the message that changes your perspective; however, you'll never find your message if you don't start. And there's no way to gain momentum if you never start.

Have you ever watched a football game and through its course the teams deliver subpar entertainment. They get the ball and get the first down. That inches along for over an hour. That is a boring game! Say in the third quarter someone makes a touchdown and in the next play a two point conversion. Then that team continues to move. They get an interception on the next possession in the end zone and run it back AAAAALLLLL the way 100 yards and they get yet another touchdown. They get that energy moving. They're looking forward to the next play quickly. First down, 2 more yards, 3 more yards, first down, TOUCHDOWN! They're failing forward. They've gained momentum from trying often. Eventually, as if in a blink of an eye, they have an additional 32 points on the scoreboard because that momentum is moving them. What happens when they start this domination? The opposing team calls an INSTANT timeout. They have to break the momentum in order to regain control of the game. They need to break their opponent's train of thought. They need the dominating team to stop for a minute instead of bulldozing over them. In that timeout that momentum breaks giving the lead a possible halt.

You have to find that momentum in your growth process. You can't stop. The journey will fucking suck! Depression doesn't just cease to exist, but don't be afraid of it. It's going to hurt. People from your past are going to look at you and judge you. They won't expect your win and many will pray for your downfall so they aren't judged for not pulling out of their own failure. But remember, none of those people are going to help you and none of those people's words are going to be able to break you in the end if you find your own momentum.

I had to accept that in order to lose the fear of failure. Failing was a sign that I was leading to achievement. A man who never fails, never grows and never achieves his goal in the end. Just as a man who fears failure will never try, leading to every goal being missed. You have a goal. I don't know what your goal is but it's there. If you take control you WILL make it through each of those failures with lessons to grow on.

My goal is to have an amazing relationship with my children. Amazing meaning they don't hate me. At 36 sitting in bankruptcy, my goal was to also get a new home and have the relationship of my dreams, which of course, required me to fail a lot and fix myself tremendously. My goal was to not be unhealthy to the point where I physically wind up killing myself due to my lack of eating, my extended stress, and the intake of what was completely taking my liver to the morgue. I'm reaching those goals. They're not happening overnight. However, they're happening a lot faster than if I had sat in the same place, the same place that many of you are sitting in while you're reading this book, knowing that you should be doing something else. Don't get me wrong, I appreciate you reading the book, but some of you are using these pages, even right now as you're reading, to procrastinate on what you have to do to achieve your win and find your freedom. If that's the case, take a break from it. Come back to the next part and let's move forward from there.

Cue awesome elevator music...

My "Break Time" - Photographed by Ty Smith of Blacksmith Digital Images

* * *

Part iii- A Step Closer

Welcome back from that small intermission. Even if it was a break just to turn the page, knowing you should have been doing something productive with yourself. No judgment here guys. I love my book too.

So, here you are. You've found hope, and you've made a decision to win. You found that a lot of people who could help you actually can't help you because only you are within yourself hearing your own cries. You've found the reality that this is still going to be a long, hard, and lonely journey. The best thing you've found is that it's a journey that you must face.

Day one of the healing process is normally easy. You hit the alarm with no snooze button and you do your planned morning ritual for your mental health. You eat a meal not consisting of a bag of chips. You exercise to burn off the alcohol and fried food that managed to somehow keep you alive all of this time. Hey, you even wash. Who on earth regularly does that when they're depressed and all is falling apart, right? You just did! Congratulations! You put on decent clothes and off you go to win your day.

Interestingly, someone notices and compliments you. "Hey, you're looking good today." You think "I've got this! I'm looking good and feeling good. Do you want to smell me? I washed today and dug out that fragrance that I love!" Day one goes by smoothly. Things that would normally frustrate you roll right off of your shoulders.

Day two hits and you do it again. Today you walk by the mirror and then you backtrack to take an actual look. You haven't looked truthfully at yourself in who knows how long until now. The small pudge that may have disgusted you last week actually has a sexy hint to it today. That workout you did yesterday is already working. You'll have a six pack in no time. Right? You actually find appreciation in your curves because hell, they're yours and you are still here to see them. Oh yeah, you have this winning thing in the bag.

This routine goes on for days, maybe even weeks to a month. Be prepared! Shit will crash and hit the fan, again. Only this time you're equipped. You have your WHY to keep you going and now you're aware that you are going to fail. No one gets it right on the first attempt and you know that now. Waiting to get back on that horse will only delay and possibly eliminate your success of freedom.

You decide how you take the new and old dark spots in your life. You now have them as a necessity to remind you not to get comfortable and that you have to celebrate those small accomplishments.

You have to continue your moving forward. Fail forward. No one can stop you and by this point you know, there is no one else to blame for not getting back up if you decide to stay down.

* * *

Part iv- Once you find yourself, you become UNSTOPPABLE

Hopefully, by this point you have found many answers within you that are opening up your path to your version of mental freedom. The world, meaning yourself, almost took you out for a long time. The blame game has finally ended and the self love is back in full effect. The ability to get back up once you have fallen has finally been put into action with some development of your mental muscle memory because you just keep on doing it like you know you have to. I'm not saying that everything from here on will be smooth sailing. However, from here on, all that you have to blame when your plan doesn't work like you planned and you don't get back up, is yourself. Don't take that as my being harsh but some of the best pills for us in life are the hardest to swallow. You decide when you don't shower. You decide when you don't brush your teeth. You decide when you go for days without properly washing our face. You decide when you don't take the moments to love YOU!

You have something pushing you. That's the knowledge that you can actually win this game now that your light is flickering back on again.

Those tiny memories of darkness that are in your mind make every small accomplishment seem that much more amazing. In those days when it all seems dark, when you get down and almost out, instead of reflecting and thinking "I always get the short end of the stick." I encourage you to, instead, reflect on those instances and think "I made it through worse and haven't been taken out yet. I can face this challenge too."

You also have a glimpse of light to guide you. That light is now within yourself and keeps you going. The only thing to do from here on is to keep the promise you made to yourself and stick to your decision of not winding up back in the backseat of that mental police car. Keep the pain in mind as a torch when you think you're about to give up. And please, by all means, when you feel as though life is pulling you back into your rut and into those dark places, REMEMBER that you have known what it feels like for "others" to hold you back. This time, they can no longer take the blame. It's all up to you. So, close your eyes, think of the dark that you've made it though, and take another bite of that perfect, golden, piece of perspective defining chicken.

* * *

Chapter 6 Questions- Step One

What's your WHY? What is that thing that keeps you going even when you don't want to. The thing that makes you take the first step out of bed every single day? Maybe it's a situation that you had to face as a child that you never want to face again (utilities being disconnected). Maybe it's your children's futures that you don't want to scar. Maybe it's to care for a family member who can no longer work for themselves. Maybe you're in a pandemic and you're the only one who can provide for your family. Down to the nitty-gritty, what is your true WHY?

-

-

-

-

-

-

-

-

How would you feel if you failed that WHY? Also, if your WHY is someone else, how would they feel if you didn't try?

-

-

-

-

-

-

-

-

-

-

-

-

-

What is was your "back seat of a police car" moment? That " I have to really fix my sh*t before I'm so far gone that there is no coming back." moment.

–

–

–

–

–

–

–

–

When will you DECIDE to win for YOURSELF?

–

(*date*)

–

(*signature*)

Chapter 7- As For Me?

*W*ell, a wise woman on the outskirts of Philadelphia once handed me a book. It introduced me to the power of the mind and your thoughts working with the Universe and all that is around you. She then told me that whatever I put into the universe will definitely come back to me. When I woke up with the belief that my days were going to be hard, that tended to be what happened. When I decided to win my day first thing in the morning, even when some or all of my plans didn't go as planned, I still came out the victor. Each and every time it stood true. Due to trial and error I've learned that when I took on the blame for all that happens in my life, good and bad, I was able to make it through all in one mental piece. That's what I now do. If I fail, I did it. If I succeed, I did it.

Flashback to when I stood in the middle of a room and screamed to my ex-wife exactly what I wanted out of a partner. Well, that happened. She showed up. I knew that partner existed the moment that I spoke of her yet I had no clue where;

however, I started to work on myself. Day in and day out and through all failure and growth, I worked on Yolanda. I was going to be prepared for when I met her and NOT for IF I met her. I had to believe. Interesting thing is, when I said that in that room, I instantly knew that the person I was speaking of was not in Pennsylvania. It was almost as though there was a beacon that went off letting me know my cries had been heard. I still believed that even if she was in the middle of hinterland, one day, she'd be standing in front of me.

While on a business trip down in Texas in 2017, 3 days after I walked away from the case working position, a young nervous woman walked up to me 14 years my junior and said "Hello. I normally don't do this, but I had to come and make sure I said hello to you before I walked out of this building because I will beat myself up for the rest of the night if I didn't." She was quiet and sincere but had found the courage to speak.

We didn't talk much farther from there for the first few months. When we looked back over our messages four months later, we realized we had been texting each other at least once a day every single day. We were already connected with no intent in the process.

Leading up to that realization, I was still working on me. My transition was at a very shaky point. Drinking was no longer what held me together constantly. It had become a pastime for social occasions. I'd started modeling to learn self confidence. My business had started to grow because the little girl inside of me, from the city, had started to trust in herself which led to some friends trusting in me as well. I had cut off all friends that were not in my story to develop me from the outside while I was working on the inside.

Jaxx was placed in my life but she wasn't for me, just yet. I learned that she rarely drank and decided that my final step to that win with her was to do the same. Of course, my doing it for her would have never worked. I would have had drinks while she wasn't around and lying would have driven a wedge that sent her right back to California if she had learned the truth. I made the decision to do it for me, for my children, and for my happiness.

On a cold November day, she came to visit me from across the country and from that point on we made conversation a daily norm. On Christmas that year, she gave me the best gift ever. She came to my state and hasn't left my side since.

There's something of a blessing about preparing yourself to win. Once you're ready, not perfect but ready, all of the blessings and wins come in a wave so tremendous that they'll have you wondering where they have been all along. You quickly start to realize that it was all at your fingertips the whole time and it was your tight grip on the past as pain that was holding it all back. It's not about that one thing that happened when you were a kid. It's not about the parents that were no longer around or the people who violated you, physically. It's about how you chose to allow those things to guide you from there after.

To this day she holds me at night when I cry, which is a rarity. She makes me food that replaces the chips and oodles of noodles that I prefer on days when my mind is still focusing on putting my left foot in front of my right and my right in front of my left. She doesn't heal the things that happen inside of my head but she allows me to heal them while I lay on her lap, without finding the need to fix things for me. She doesn't belittle my strength my leading me to believe that it is her who fixes me. We both know that without my decision no change would come. She never fights with me, like legit, I've never heard her raise her voice at me. She never touches me to bring me harm. She lets me go for only TWO days without showering and taking care of myself before she lovingly tells me "Hey babe. The waters running."

It's been three years since that December. My ex-wife finally signed the papers releasing me from her matrimonial bond allowing me to completely give my heart to my newfound love. Within three weeks of my divorce we married and I was blessed to be given away by my oldest daughter. Yup, that daughter that I thought I had lost, she loves me too.

Even though my youngest daughter lives with her other mother full time, in a separate life from mine, my birth children and I smile every single day at each other. I saw my granddaughter born in December of 2019 and was blessed to assist in the breast feeding process. My children are happy. They are loved by me and most importantly, BY THEMSELVES. They are learning the power of selflove and that is the best gift I have ever been able to give them. Each day, I'm moving a few steps closer to them being able to live a life where I am irrelevant to their daily growth.

I don't remember my mother's voice. My grandmother's laughs are only heard in my imagination while I look at pictures of her. My grandfather and her other son's, Carlos and Angel, have joined her and my father as memories. I'm happy believing that they are all celebrating my life with me, on a daily.

Today, I'm typing this from a balcony overlooking palm trees on the far East Coast of Puerto Rico. My father's native land has now become my family's sanctuary. Y el Español se esta convirtiendo lenta pero seguramente en mi segundo idioma.

Yup, (*Spanish is slowly but surely becoming my second language*). Apparently, that was my job to learn as well.

While I'm still healing, the only force keeping me from wanting to leave my pillow in the morning is the fact that, for as long as she'll have me, I don't want to move from laying next to her. My wife supports my growth and she has become a part of my WHY.

I've also made the decision of full forgiveness. I've forgiven my past. I've forgiven myself for blaming others for my reactions and gained the awareness that those were still my actions that I chose to respond with. My children and I have fallen in love with each other again; the way we loved when they were first born and I used to hold them in my arms and breathe in their baby yawns.

Now that I've decided to win, I'm blessed to believe that I'll never have to picture those lonely days again be it with or without my loved ones present. For the first time in my almost 40 years I've developed an appreciation for myself and know that being alone doesn't make me lonely. I am my own best friend through thick and thin and I'll cherish that until I leave this form. In that, I've truly found my light in the midst of this mess. It was me all along.

Now that you've read this and have answered to yourself, I pray that you too are developing a sense of peace and direction within YOU. You are powerful beyond your own belief. You hold the key to the gates that are blocking you from your freedom. NO ONE, not a single person, can take away your joy once you decide it resides within you. It's not theirs. IT'S YOURS and yours alone.

I send you off with hope, many blessings, and the true belief that in this world where we are all an orphan within ourselves, you have decided that you too, are FOUND.

My Jaxx and I

Puddin, FOUND!

* * *

Chapter 7 Question- You FOUND

What are you neglecting within yourself? (hair, skin, diet, teeth, passions…)

-

-

-

-

-

-

-

-

-

-

-

How, in detail, do you see your FOUND? Or as I was so bluntly asked, "WHAT IN THE Fu$& DO YOU WANT?"

-

-

-

-

-

-

-

-

-

-

-

-

-

https://www.facebook.com/Yolanda-M-Rodriguez-104864561557879/

Chapter 7- As For Me?

Email- authoryolandarodriguez@gmail.com

Chapter 8- The Best Part Thus Far! YOU-From your darkness to your LIGHT (Fill this section in from the questions asked in the prior chapters.)

Chapter 1 Questions- The Outer Shell

*W*ho are you? I know that question can be used very loosely but when you look in the mirror you see who you BELIEVE you are. Are you a parent? Are you a business partner? Are you a college student? Are you a teacher? When you look at you, WHO ARE YOU?

\-

\-

\-

\-

\-

\-

\-

When you were a child what did you want to be when you grew up? Dump all of those dreams here.

\-

\-

\-

\-

\-

\-

Chapter 2 Questions- From A Place Of Love

Who were your childhood "Angels" that you found to be your protectors? (a guardian, a friend, a teacher, a stuffed animal, a pet)

-

-

-

-

-

What did these Angels help you through?

-

-

-

-

Chapter 3 Questions- Hello Inner You. I'm Listening...

I told you my story to open your heart. I wanted to have a conversation with your child within. Usually this child is hiding behind blame, guilt, or avoidance. However you're still there and I'm glad you came out to join us. Namaste, The divine in me respectfully recognizes the divine in you.

What situations in your life is that inner child sitting behind? What are the "If only my mother would have" or the "If I wouldn't have had... happen to me", maybe even the "If I didn't look like (...) then the other kids wouldn't have..." situations that you are holding onto ever so dearly. The ones that you are holding onto so much so, that they are hindering your growth? Talk to me, inner child.

–

–

–

–

–

–

–

What do you believe those situations and events are holding you back from today?

-

-

-

-

-

How are they holding you back? (mental health, alcoholism, fear, etc.…)

-

-

-

-

-

-

-

Chapter 4 Questions- Survival Mode

What were some of the escape tactics you used in your younger years to dilute the negative things you were experiencing, literally or mentally?

-

-

-

-

-

-

-

-

When you left your childhood home either physically or mentally, headed towards your next goal, what was your BIG plan? I'm not asking you what you wanted to be when you grew up. I'm asking what you were truthfully going to do? What, from your past, were you grateful to finally make a change to?

If you haven't left yet, what is your plan/thing that you want to make different in your next chapter?

-

-

-

-

-

-

-

-

How does that plan differ from where you are now or does it?

-

-

-

-

-

-

-

If you are not where you planned to be, do you believe you are more pleased with your current outcome or do you feel like you failed with that goal?

If you haven't started that path yet, what's an alternate outcome you will be pleased with if life doesn't go exactly as planned?

–

–

–

–

–

–

Who do you blame/congratulate for those plans working out or completely flopping? What was your role?

–

–

–

–

Chapter 5 Questions- The Blame Game

Who do you charge not fixing the you that you sit with today? Trust me we all blame someone. They walked into your life, you thought they would be the end to the inner trauma, and yet you still hear your OWN words reminding you otherwise. The cries inside still ring out to you. Who walked out the door and never returned? They may be the one that you call who listens but cannot fix it all. That person might be laying next to you while you are reading this. Don't worry, I won't tell them.

You can also add in here why you thought they'd be able to change/help you? What did they have that you were lacking that you believed would be, in some form, your saving grace?

–

–

–

–

–

–

–

What are the bad habits that you have perfected that you KNOW you need to break? The routines and tendencies that you use to drown out the inner noise and may even, at times, hide from those around you.

–

–

–

–

–

–

–

–

–

–

–

–

What are these practices holding you back from achieving?
   ex: "If I stopped hitting that snooze button I could...."

-

-

-

-

-

-

-

-

Chapter 6 Questions- Step One

What's your WHY? What is that thing that keeps you going even when you don't want to. The thing that makes you take the first step out of bed every single day? Maybe it's a situation that you had to face as a child that you never want to face again (utilities being disconnected). Maybe it's your children's futures that you don't want to scar. Maybe it's to care for a family member who can no longer work for themselves. Maybe you're in a pandemic and you're the only one who can provide for your family. Down to the nitty-gritty, what's your true WHY?

\-

\-

\-

\-

\-

\-

\-

\-

\-

\-

\-

\-

\-

How would you feel if you failed that WHY? Also, if your WHY is someone else, how would they feel if you didn't try?

-

-

-

-

-

-

What is was your "back seat of a police car" moment? That " I have to really fix my sh*t before I'm so far gone that there is no coming back." moment.

-

-

-

-

-

Chapter 7- You FOUND

What are you neglecting within yourself? (hair, skin, diet, teeth, passions...)

-

-

-

-

-

-

-

-

-

-

-

-

How, in detail, do you see your FOUND? Or as I was so bluntly asked, "WHAT IN THE F*$& DO YOU WANT?"

-

-

-

-

-

-

-

-

-

-

-

-

-

-

Chapter 8 Question- The Truth

After seeing your greatness within and knowing that you can bring it to the surface, how do you feel about your future compared to before you started answering these questions to yourself?

-

-

-

-

-

-

-

-

Now that you've written this all here, read it aloud to yourself. For once, answer to YOU. It will be hard to admit the things that you already know within aloud to yourself. However, without doing so you'll find yourself picking this book up in a year or so, scratching out your "decide" date and attempting to start over again.

You already hold greatness. It lives within you. You were born with it and it did not die simply because you hid it away in a closet to get covered in mental dust and fog. Your greatness was misplaced and put on a temporary hold. Your past is currently residing solely in your mind and your current is yours to change. I beg you to please let the world and yourself see your greatness. Just as I learned over time that I am worth it, YOU are worth it.

I beg of you to show the world, and most importantly, show yourself,

that you are FOUND.

#ShowGreat

https://www.facebook.com/Yolanda-M-Rodriguez-104864561557879/

Email- authoryolandarodriguez@gmail.com

ig- rodriguezyo